FROM DARKNESS INTO LIGHT

My Journey

MARK BUCKLEY

Published by
Mark Buckley Ministries
www.markbuckleyministries.com

ISBN 978-1-7330163-0-8

Printed in the United States of America

Book Design, Back Cover, and editing by: Margie Wilson
margiewilson@getyourwordsworth.com

Front Cover design and layout by: Pat McCornack
patmac@novato.net

April 2020 Printing

To obtain more copies of this book or to contact Mark:
Mark Buckley Ministries
7000 North Central Avenue
Phoenix, AZ 85020
mark@markbuckleyministries.com
OR order from Amazon.com

I dedicate this book to Kristina.

She has been at my side as a faithful wife and great friend since 1973. Kristina married a carpenter who ended up becoming a pastor. This required her to make some major adjustments. She is able to discover God's Kingdom in nature and with the people she loves. She can cook, sew, quilt, deliver babies, teach the Word, fix computers, grow a garden, catch fish, clean elk, and care for the sick.

Kristina is an amazing wife, mother, Nana, and friend. I love being with her and thank God for the privilege of sharing our lives together. Many of our adventures have been too wild and personal for me to include in this book. May God bless you with a spouse who brings you joy like she has brought to me.

This is the story of my transformation from a confused teenager indulging in danger to a man with purpose and destiny.

Mark Buckley

TABLE OF CONTENTS

PART ONE

FROM ALL-AMERICAN BOY TO MENTAL PATIENT

INTRODUCTION

A blaring voice came over the intercom into our dorm room. It woke me from a foggy dream. "Good morning, gentlemen! It is 6:00 A.M., February 16, 1969, and time to get up!"

The voice boomed a second time. "Good morning, gentlemen! It is 6:00 A.M., February 16, 1969. It's time to get up!"

The men in the beds around me struggled to awaken and sit up. We were all in a drug-induced stupor, caused by the medications we were given twice daily. One stooped man dragged himself past me to the bathroom, doing the "Thorazine shuffle."

Like many at Napa State Hospital in 1969, I was taking Thorazine, the medication they gave to psychotic hippies and delusional people. Under the influence of Thorazine, my brain felt like it was covered with a damp washrag, preventing creative thoughts from penetrating my mind, and joy from entering my heart. It was like an anti-LSD. I had lost all sense of meaning and purpose.

I was nineteen years old. I should have been waking up in a college dorm room like many of my friends. I should have been excited about life, and girls, and learning new things. What made life worth living was a distant memory that I could no longer grasp.

I could have been waking up in the jungles of Vietnam, like others from my high school. Then again, some of them who had been drafted would never wake up in this world again. That reality was part of the reason I was in Napa State Hospital.

This is the story of how my seemingly normal life went off the rails and how it eventually became something more purposeful than I could have ever imagined.

I was a pastor in three different churches from 1973–2019. I now serve many churches and leaders. I often illustrate my teachings with stories from my life. I have been sharing many of these stories publicly for more than forty years.

I learned an important lesson early in my ministry. If I realize a teacher or pastor embellishes, exaggerates, or lies, I lose trust in the person and discount the veracity of anything else he or she says. Pastors without integrity lose their effectiveness in ministry. I never want to lose people's trust.

There may be a few inaccuracies in this book, i.e., I may have the names of two hobos wrong. However, most of the people I mention are still alive and can verify what I have written. They may have slightly different memories of these events, but their names have not been altered and the events really happened.

Many great friends and stories were edited out of this book. Please forgive me if I did not mention you, or if I offended you by what I wrote.

CHAPTER ONE

MY EARLY YEARS

If you had known my family and me in my childhood, you probably would not have predicted I would become a mental patient. In many ways, I grew up as an all-American boy.

I was born in 1950 in San Francisco at Stanford Hospital, the first child of John and Roberta Buckley. My dad was a dedicated Roman Catholic who attended Mass every Sunday. He played football and basketball with passion and worked in a grocery store for twenty-five cents an hour. He went to Catholic schools and graduated from St. James High School and the University of San Francisco. He left USF for three years to join the Air Force to fight in World War II in Europe. When he returned, he finished USF and married Roberta Mathews. Before the war, they had met at a dance at Rio Nido, on the Russian River when they were both 16. My dad then graduated from USF law school, flunked the bar exam three times, and began a career in banking.

My mom was raised a nominal Episcopalian, attending Christmas and Easter services. However, she was so impressed with her husband's commitment to the church that she began classes after my birth and became a Catholic.

She took her new faith in the church's teachings on everything, including birth control, very seriously. Consequently, as the years went by and we moved from San Francisco across the Golden Gate Bridge to Terra Linda, in Marin County, one Buckley baby after another was born. By the time I started Terra Linda High School in 1964, I was the oldest of eight children—four boys and four girls.

Roman Catholic Teaching

Being Roman Catholic was a big part of my identity growing up. Our family attended Mass every Sunday, even when we went on vacation. Starting in first grade, my mother made sure I went to catechism classes every week during the school year. Through these classes I came to believe in Jesus Christ. I went to confession every few weeks, so that I could partake in communion with a clear conscience.

I always felt cleansed after confessing my sins to the priest when I was young.

Unfortunately, as I got older, I found myself confessing the same sins every time I went to confession. I would talk in church services. I was selfish. I was often mean to my younger brothers and sisters. I picked on weaker kids in school. No matter how much I wanted to be a better person, and how many times I confessed these sins, my behavior never changed for longer than a few days.

One Saturday night a few days before Christmas when I was thirteen years old, I had a troubled heart and knew I needed to go to confession. One of my friends had given me a *Playboy* magazine. I didn't take time to look at it when he first gave it to me. I took it home and hid it under the pillow on my bed.

That night, I waited until my brother Barry was asleep in our bedroom and everything was quiet in our house. Then, I quietly turned on the lamp beside my bed and slipped the *Playboy* out from under my pillow. I had just opened it when my bedroom door burst open.

Mom was standing in the doorway. She demanded, "What is that? What are you doing with that!" With a look of disgust, she ripped the *Playboy* out of my hands, turned, walked out, and shut the door. That was the only time in my life I remember my mother opening the door to my room at night. Somehow, she knew I was doing something wrong. It wouldn't be the last time her gift of discernment would manifest when I was heading for trouble.

After she left, I concluded that since my mother knew what I had done, then the Lord knew what I had done. So, I had to go to confession.

The Saturday night before Christmas was a busy night for confessions at St. Vincent's Catholic Church. [Our parish, St. Isabella's, was using St. Vincent's sanctuary while our new church was being built in Terra Linda.] Long lines of people waited to enter each of the confession booths. Then I spotted a much shorter line on the far side of the altar. I walked over and got behind four or five other people. While I waited, I began to mull over the sins I knew I had to confess. I was conflicted. I had been taught in catechism class that you must confess all your sins if you want forgiveness. I wanted forgiveness, but I hated to tell the priest about the Playboy. Since confession was anonymous, I decided I would tell everything to the priest.

About the time I resolved to confess everything, the person ahead of me in line returned from his confession and it was my turn to walk around the corner of the altar. As I turned the corner, I entered a large room. I saw a priest just sitting in a folding chair right out in the open. There was an empty chair next to him.

What had I been thinking? No wonder the line had been shorter than all the other lines. There was no confession booth! No anonymity! We were right out in the open. For the first time in my life, the priest could see who I was as I made my confession. I wanted to turn and run away. The priest saw me hesitate and motioned for me to sit down.

I sat down in the chair like a lamb about to be slaughtered. The priest could sense my fear. He turned his chair to the side and looked straight ahead, as if he would now provide me some privacy. "You can begin," he declared in a deep voice.

"Bless me, father, for I have sinned," I began as I made the sign of the cross. "It has been about a month since my last confession." I caught my breath. "I have been mean to my brothers and sisters. We have talked in church." I was suddenly glad I could confess these sins one more time. I continued and confessed each trivial offense I could remember. Then I paused.

"Ahem." The priest cleared his throat. He sensed I wasn't finished. It was his way of saying, "Spit it out kid. Tell me what's really going on." The moment felt dark and heavy.

I whispered, "And . . . I looked at a *Playboy*. . . ."

"You what?" he yelled as he turned and looked right at me.

"Just a few pages," I pleaded, with my head down. I was desperate to find mercy. I knew a spiritual death sentence was justified.

He realized he had traumatized me and turned his head back

to the side. "Continue."

"That's all. These are my sins," I whimpered.

He gave me penance. I don't remember how many Hail Marys and Our Fathers the priest required for this penance. But I said them all twice, because I really wanted forgiveness and never wanted to have to confess something this serious again.

One winter weekend, our family went skiing at Lake Tahoe with my godfather, Owen Sullivan, and his family. We were caught in a major snowstorm. The snow was so deep that we couldn't drive to the nearest Catholic church for Mass. Instead, that Sunday, my dad and Owen took our families to an Episcopal church a few blocks away from Owen's cabin. They told us it was the closest thing to the Catholic church, and the Lord would understand our situation.

It was my first experience going to a church of a different denomination. I couldn't help but compare this church to St. Isabella's. Their building was clean and neat, but not as big as our church back home. They had a few stained glass windows, but not as many or as big as ours. Their service was longer than our usual thirty-five-minute Mass. Their liturgy used familiar words, but the congregation didn't seem enthusiastic about it. And, their communion wafer didn't taste authentic.

I was intrigued but not overly impressed with my first venture outside our tradition. The most memorable effect of this experience was my father's comment, "The Lord will understand our situation." It seemed liberating.

Shortly thereafter, in a catechism class one evening, I asked our teacher a question about God. He replied, "That is a mystery." Then he continued his lecture. I was left thinking. "If it is a mystery to you, and a mystery to me, I'm going to go somewhere where I can find some answers."

That was my last catechism class; afterward, my attendance at Sunday Mass became sporadic. When I turned sixteen, my parents let me make my own decision about church attendance, and most Sundays, I chose not to go to church.

Going to Europe with Grandma Mathews

I loved playing sports from the time I was a young boy. My friends and I played football, baseball, and basketball in their seasons, both in school and after school every day. At fourteen, I was pitching for our Senior League baseball team. I threw a curve ball that made batters jump out of the batter's box before it broke over the plate for a strike.

In the Spring of 1964, I was dominating the league, until Grandma Mathews took me to Europe for six weeks. My grandpa, Arthur Mathews, had died from a stroke a few weeks earlier, and to help cope with her grief, Grandma decided to go on a tour of Europe and take me with her. I didn't like leaving during baseball season, but the trip was a great opportunity to travel.

Cecily Mathews, my maternal grandmother, was a salty Englishwoman. She and I had a special relationship. She took me on a train to Reno when I was ten years old. We stayed at Harrah's Hotel so she could play the slot machines in its casino.

Grandma loved Pall Mall cigarettes, Scotch whisky, gambling, and me. She taught me to play poker at home and always encouraged me to give her a quarter to play the slot machines when she went to Reno. She would always give me a $7.50 jackpot she won in return for my quarters, so it was a no-brainer to invest with her.

Grandma and I took a first-class trip to Europe. We flew to Copenhagen and then went by train to Wiesbaden, Venice, Rome, Florence, and Paris. We took the ferry to London and then the train to Edinburgh. We attended the Folies Bergère in Paris and the best theater productions in London. We stayed in fancy hotels and ate in the some of the best restaurants in Europe. I had many great meals, but after six weeks of restaurant food three times a day, I was glad to get back to my mom's home cooking. I have had no desire to eat at expensive restaurants since that trip.

Returning to Terra Linda in June after our trip, I immediately started pitching two games a week for our baseball team. My curve ball still had a wicked break, but six weeks without working out cost me dearly. By the middle of the second game I pitched, my right elbow was hurting badly. I pitched through the pain. By the second week, my elbow hurt so badly I could barely grip a baseball bat. The ligaments in my elbow were so torn that I never pitched again.

In September, I went to high school, looking forward to new adventures and playing sports on another level.

Sports at Terra Linda High

At Terra Linda High School, so many guys went out for the football, basketball, and baseball teams, the coaches had to hold tryouts for each sport. Many boys' dreams were shattered when the coaches put their names on the cut list posted on the locker room wall.

I made first string on each team and went to practice or games every day after school during my freshman year. However, never getting to go home and get a snack after school all year was exhausting. I continued playing football and baseball but dropped basketball after my freshman year.

I did well in both sports. I played third base and center field on our baseball team. I made first team All-League my senior year, but my damaged elbow prevented me from pursuing my dream of becoming a professional baseball player.

In football, I was the team's punter, kick-off man, wide receiver, half back, and safety. I was the leading ground gainer in the Marin County Athletic League my senior year. I hated our intense practices, but I stayed with football because I loved having my name in the newspapers, stands full of fans at the games, and the attention, especially from the girls at Shakey's Pizza after our games.

We lost only one game my senior year—by two points, when I stepped on the back of the end zone line for a safety while attempting to punt. Afterward, the crowd at Shakey's was subdued. Some of the same people who usually treated me like a hero shunned me. I realized how shallow those friendships were.

This gave me a hunger for deeper relationships. I wanted friendships based on real love, not temporary success. This hunger soon led me into the hippie movement, which was starting to flourish in California.

CHAPTER TWO

DESCENDING INTO THE COUNTERCULTURE

Festivals and Concerts

In June of 1967 I attended the Magic Mountain Music Festival on Mount Tamalpais, which is considered the first-ever rock festival in America. Thousands of young people were bussed up to the amphitheater on top of the large tree-covered mountain that overlooks Marin County. The bands had come from around the country, and stoned guys and girls danced around the stage.

My hair was still short because baseball season had just ended. The girls seemed attracted to the long-haired, stoned guys wearing tie-dyed shirts. Joints were passed from person to person throughout the crowd. I tried smoking a joint, but I couldn't hold the marijuana in my lungs without coughing it up. That's when I decided to start smoking cigarettes, so I could prepare my lungs to hold down the weed.

Shortly after that, I went to a concert at The Fillmore with two of my friends. We got drunk on vodka before the concert. It seemed like everyone else was using marijuana or LSD. So, I learned to get high on marijuana. In the following months, I went to concerts and danced to Jimi Hendrix, The Who, The Jefferson Airplane, The Grateful Dead, Janis Joplin, Jeff Beck, Cream, Chicago, and every other big-name band that played at The Fillmore, Avalon Ballroom, or Winterland in San Francisco. Almost everyone, including me, got stoned at those concerts.

Timothy Leary and LSD

One night I was listening to a talk radio show at home with my dad. Timothy Leary was being interviewed. He was talking about turning on, tuning in, and dropping out. He claimed that LSD allowed people to explore the inner space of their minds and expand their consciousness. He seemed articulate and intelligent, and his message made sense. Why wouldn't everyone want to explore and expand their consciousness?

Soon after, I read an article in the *San Francisco Chronicle* about LSD. The writer interviewed hippies, who comprised a new culture of people living in communes, sharing food, sex, and LSD. Their lifestyle intrigued me.

At the same time, I felt pressure because of the Vietnam War. The fighting was escalating with more Vietnamese and Americans being killed every day. Some of my classmates had already enlisted in the Army and others would eventually be drafted. I wanted no part in killing people in a war I didn't think was wise for America.

It seemed like I had a choice between becoming a hippie or a soldier. I chose being a hippie. I didn't realize at the time that eventually there would be more American casualties from the sex, drugs, and rock-and-roll lifestyle than the Vietnam War. And I would be one of them.

Hitchhiking with Larry

Larry Bresnan attended Novato High, but he became my friend our senior year. We had known each other since our Pop Warner football days. We met up again at a dance in Novato and started spending time together. He was the first person I was able to talk with on the phone for long periods of time. We enjoyed going on double dates, though we often talked to each other more than the girls we were dating.

On a couple of weekends in 1968, Larry and I hitchhiked down to Big Sur and slept on the beach. Another time we hitchhiked up the coast to Mendocino and built a big driftwood bonfire on the beach.

In the late 1960s, it was easy to get rides hitchhiking in California. Young people were pouring in from every part of the country, looking for the love they heard about in songs on the radio. Almost everyone who picked us up either offered us marijuana or accepted a joint from the stash we carried with us.

Larry and I had planned to travel to Europe after graduating from high school. But in June when we graduated and it was time for us to go, Larry told me he didn't have enough money saved for the trip. I was very disappointed, but we decided to hitchhike to Seattle instead.

As we hitchhiked up Highway 101, we spent a night in a rescue mission on the outskirts of Eureka. To get the free dinner and a place to sleep, we had to listen to a gospel presentation. The presentation started with three people leading gospel songs; they seemed to be right out of the early 1950s and did not impress me. I tried not to laugh at the guys who wore trousers with rolled-up cuffs and the woman with permed hair, wearing a long dress.

We made it to Portland where there was a budding hippie scene. We began hanging around coffee shops and bookstores downtown. We stayed in a commune, practiced meditation, participated in a séance, and got stoned every day. One night we attended a draft-card burning at a local church with Joan Baez and David Harris. Joan was a folk music icon and David was a fiery anti-war activist. I agreed with their message, but I was cautious. I hated the Vietnam War, but the idea of defying the draft system seemed dangerous to me.

There were a lot of available girls in Portland, but after a couple of weeks I became restless. Something about the hippie lifestyle was leaving me feeling empty. Larry and I agreed to split up. He stayed in Portland and I decided to head to Seattle.

Freight Train to Seattle

Seattle was a challenging destination because hitchhiking in Washington state was illegal. I had heard the best way to get to Seattle was to jump a freight train. In hindsight, thinking this was a good way to travel 200 miles seems foolish. However, when I was 18 years old, adventure triumphed over safety and sanity.

So, carrying my backpack, I hitchhiked to the train yard outside Portland and started walking among the idle trains. The guys on the street who had advised me to jump a train had warned me to watch out for train company detectives who patrolled the rail yards.

As I wandered through the yard, there were trains on several tracks but few people. Finally, I saw a man in overalls who looked like a worker. I asked him if there was a train heading to Seattle anytime soon. He pointed me toward a long freight train and suggested I hide in some bushes near the train until the detectives did their boxcar inspection.

I walked alongside the train until I found some large bushes. Nobody was in sight, so I pushed my way through the branches and sat down to wait. Suddenly, through the leaves, I saw two men walking beside the train. They stopped several times to climb up on boxcars and peer inside. I assumed they were the detectives. I wondered what would happen if they caught me trying to hop aboard the train. My heart was racing as they walked past the bushes without stopping.

Soon after they passed, I heard a whistle and the train started to move. I didn't see anyone around, so I crawled out of the bushes. The train was moving slowly, but all its cargo doors were shut. I wondered how I could get on it. As it began to gain speed, a red boxcar with open doors moved past me. I decided to try to jump inside. I began to jog alongside it and threw my backpack up into the boxcar. I grabbed the handrail and then jumped on to the metal steps and climbed into the empty boxcar. I had made it aboard.

Within a minute, I was stunned.

From the other side of the tracks, two men pulled themselves up and crawled into the boxcar with me. They were scruffy-looking guys with nothing other than a gallon wine jug between them. I realized they were hobos, whom I had heard about but had never seen. They stood up and smiled like we were long lost friends who had arranged to meet this way. I didn't know if I could trust them or if they would rob me the first chance they got.

The train continued to pick up speed. I sat down next to my

pack and stared out through the open door. We were traveling through the green countryside of southern Washington. The hobos were passing their wine back and forth, taking big swigs out of the bottle. They asked me if I wanted a drink. It didn't look appealing, but I wanted to seem friendly. I accepted the gallon jug, took a sip of the cheap wine, and handed it back.

They kept chugging the bottle and were soon laughing loudly. I don't remember for sure, but their names may have been Jimmy and Bill. Bill was the older of the two and wore a dirty flannel shirt and grubby jeans. He asked me where I was going. When I told him, he wondered why I wanted to go to Seattle. I told him I was traveling around the country for the first time.

Jimmy stood up and brought the wine over to me again. He pressed his face near mine and slurred his words, but I still remember his message: "Kid, this traveling is no life for you. You need to settle down and get a job and have a family. It's dangerous out on the road."

Suddenly, Bill started yelling and struggled to his feet. "What the hell are you talking about? You never settled down and had no family! Leave that kid alone! He needs to see the world."

Jimmy turned to face him. "Don't you go telling me nothin'. I'll tell this kid what I damn well please, and you don't get nothin' to say about it!"

Bill staggered across the boxcar toward the two of us. "Listen, kid. You gotta see the world. It's a big world and you gotta see it all. That's the only way to live."

Jimmy stared at me. "He don't know shit. He never done anything."

Bill grabbed Jimmy's arm and spun him around, "You don't go talking to that kid that way! You hear me?!"

Jimmy pressed his chest against Bill's. "I'll talk to that kid any way I damn well please! What ya gonna do about it? The kid needs a family!"

Bill threw his arms around Jimmy and tried to throw him down. Jimmy fought back. The train was lurching as they bearhugged each other in a drunken embrace. They finally fell to the boxcar floor. I stood in fear as they wrestled and rolled across the car in each other's arms. They rolled up to the far side of the car. Suddenly, they stopped rolling and fighting. They lay still. They had passed out in each other's arms.

I sat back down and stared through the open boxcar doors. Cozy farmhouses were starting to light up as families gathered for dinner. I contemplated my future as the train moved north: *Was it best to settle down now or keep traveling until I found peace in my soul?*

Then I fell asleep. I awoke as the train pulled into Seattle. Jimmy and Bill woke up as well. They stood up without acknowledging me and jumped down to the ground as the train slowed down. They walked away without saying good-bye. It wouldn't be the last time I would see addicts act like different people when they were no longer stoned. Those were not the kind of friends I wanted. I wasn't sure I would ever find the answers I was looking for, but I was determined to keep searching.

I hung out in Seattle for a few days in the emerging hippie scene around the University of Washington. I borrowed a guitar and sat on the university lawns plucking at the strings and trying to attract one of the many girls who were drawn to guys with long hair, beads, and sandals. My guitar playing was primitive, and my singing was worse. After a few futile days, I decided to head home. I put out my thumb at a freeway on-ramp knowing it was illegal to hitchhike in Washington, but I soon got a ride.

Within a few days, I was back in Marin. There I learned that my friend Andy McIntire had formed a rock band with a couple of our high school friends. I went to listen to them practice. They thought they were destined to be as big as The Beatles one day. I had my doubts. I was stoned but not that delusional.

CHAPTER THREE

SEEING THE COUNTRY

Andy had a Volkswagen van and he wanted to take a trip across the country. It wasn't exactly like going to Europe, but it sounded like the next best thing, so I decided to go with him.

From Marin, we drove toward Los Angeles and then headed east through Las Vegas. We were too young to gamble, so we kept going to the Grand Canyon. We arrived at the North Rim of the canyon in the late afternoon, just as dark storm clouds were gathering over the rim. We pulled into a parking lot and a thunderstorm broke loose. Rain poured down on the van, shaking us with its ferocity. Within a few minutes, it stopped, and we climbed out of the van.

A bright rainbow appeared suspended over the canyon a few hundred yards across the parking lot. We walked toward the rainbow, climbed over a rail fence, and approached the edge of the canyon. I'm afraid of heights, but the sight before us was breathtaking.

From the van, the rainbow had appeared as a semicircle with its edges resting on the horizon. As we peered down into the canyon, thousands of feet below us, the rainbow formed a full circle. We were stunned by the radiance of the rainbow. It had never occurred to me it was possible for a rainbow to form a full circle. It was a sign with meaning I would not comprehend for many years.

Andy and I didn't want to spend the money to stay at the hotel on the North Rim, so we piled back in his van and continued to head east.

Our next stop was Gallup, New Mexico. For hours the freeway signs had read, "Gallup 245 miles, Gallup 190 miles, Gallup 75 miles," etc. I was anticipating a special city. However, in 1968, Gallup was a dusty old town with not much happening.

My main memory of Gallup was seeing big cockroaches in the house where we spent the night. We had met some guys around our age at a local store when we stopped for gas. Andy had longer hair than me and he seemed really cool to teenagers everywhere we went. When we asked these guys if they had a place where we could "crash" for the night, they gladly welcomed us.

Our Gallup experience was typical of our entire trip as we drove east. We had sleeping bags with us, so we occasionally camped out. We never paid for a motel room. Whenever we stopped in a city, we searched for kids who looked like they wanted to become hippies. We would start talking with them and let them know we were from San Francisco and heading across the country. They would offer us food and a free place to stay.

By the time we reached New Orleans, we had perfected the art of leveraging our status. The middle of the country was a few years behind California when it came to the counterculture experience. Hippies came from San Francisco, and kids across America wanted to meet hippies. The kids we met wanted to know all about the rock scene in San Francisco. We were happy to oblige them for food and a free place to stay.

In New Orleans, we spent several days living in an old Southern mansion. You could drink alcohol legally at eighteen in Louisiana. I went to a nearby café to drink beer and play chess with the locals. On one day, I lost several intense chess games to a gifted player. No matter what the game, I have always hated to lose.

Next, we stopped in Kent, Mississippi, in a poor section of town, where we received a surprising welcome. A family was sitting on the porch of their little worn house when we parked and walked toward a small store across the street. Three kids scrambled off their porch and ran up to us.

"Are you The Beatles?" they asked breathlessly.

We started to laugh until we realized they weren't joking. We didn't realize young white men with long hair didn't stop in this section of Kent very often. We were instant celebrities.

The kids grabbed our hands and pulled us over to meet their parents on the porch.

The adults stood up and insisted we have dinner with them. We were soon drinking beer and telling them stories about California. We passed on the temptation to pretend we were The Beatles.

We also passed on their offer to spend the night in their house. This family had a lot of love. It wasn't the free love of the hippies, but love that came from a heart to welcome strangers. It was compelling to feel the love and acceptance of African Americans who lived in a segregated community. They already had what hippies were striving for. After dinner, we continued to travel east.

Adventures in New York City

Andy and I eventually reached New York City. We were planning to stay with friends of his family. There, on a busy four-lane roadway, Andy was attempting to change lanes on a curve as we went under an overpass. He asked me if the right lane was clear. I cast a cursory glance over my right shoulder and answered, "Yes." As Andy pulled the van into the right lane, we were struck in the side by a car I hadn't noticed. We skidded to a stop after smashing against the other car and blocked traffic in the right lane.

The van was badly damaged and had to be towed to a garage. After that, Andy and I took a cab to the high-rise on Fifth Avenue where the friends of his family lived in a penthouse apartment. We stayed with them for a couple of days while we explored the city. Andy decided to fly home to California when he found out it would take a couple of weeks for his van to be repaired.

The evening Andy left, his friends also left the city, so I found myself walking the streets needing a place to stay. It was after 10:00 P.M. when I wandered into Greenwich Village. I stopped in a city park where I heard music coming from a stage. Several hundred people were gathered listening to Frank Zappa and The Mothers of Invention. I became fixated by one line from a song they sang, "In the bowling alley of your mind, I'll be your pin boy."

I wasn't stoned, but my mind was scrambling to figure out where I was going to spend the night. Then I noticed a long-haired guy with his girlfriend sitting on the grass. I walked over to them and said hello. We talked as the music continued to play. When the concert ended around midnight, they asked me if I needed a place to stay. I told them my situation and accepted their invitation to stay with them.

We walked through Greenwich Village along sidewalks with hippies, drug addicts, drag queens, and street people mingling in a midnight milieu of humanity. We eventually arrived at an abandoned old tenement building with a chain on the front door. The guy pushed the door open as far as the chain would allow. The girl squeezed through into the darkened entryway. We followed. Fortunately, my backpack turned sideways was able to make it as well.

I spent the next few days staying in this building. It had been condemned by the building inspectors who placed the chain on the entry door. My most vivid memory of this apartment was seeing two large cockroaches scurry out of a bowl of brown rice that my host, the long-haired man, handed me for dinner the next night. He didn't seem too concerned about them, so who was I to decline to eat what they served me? Besides, I was on a tight budget.

I did splurge one day on a Robin Hood-style hat with a large feather. New York City made me feel anonymous. There were thousands of people on the streets night and day. Wearing the hat while I explored the city made me feel unique.

I went to Coney Island. I rode the Staten Island Ferry for five cents. We passed the Statue of Liberty, which loomed large in the harbor. I walked through Central Park. I watched guys playing chess in Washington Square. I rode the subway one afternoon, and when I exited, I saw Black people everywhere. I realized I was in the middle of Harlem. It was unsettling to feel so different from everyone around me. I had my first taste of what many African Americans living in a white society must feel every day.

After a few days, I felt it was time to leave New York. I had a high school friend who lived in Rhode Island. I decided to go visit him until Andy's van was repaired and we could resume our trip.

I said good-bye to my hosts in Greenwich Village and hitchhiked out of the city. I was picked up by a teenager who lived with his parents and two sisters. They welcomed me into their big house on Long Island. We spent the day at the beach and played poker that night with his sisters and their friends.

One sister was a blond and the other a brunette. Their personalities were as different as their looks. One of them loved life and wanted to stay up all night savoring each experience and squeezing the most out of every day. The other said she loved to sleep. She said good sleep enabled her to stay healthy and get the most out of every day.

I've remembered these sisters because my approach to life and sleep followed the first sister's philosophy until I got into trouble in midlife, and then I gradually switched to the second sister's approach.

On to New England

From Long Island, I hitchhiked to Connecticut, where I was picked up by a couple on their way to a bluegrass festival. I joined hundreds of people at the festival and danced in the meadow in front of the stage. I felt like I was back home in California. Afterward, I spent the night with some guys who had a house near the festival. It was more like a bachelor pad than the hippie commune they aspired to become.

Leaving Connecticut, my next ride took me to Boston. Boston seemed crowded like New York City, so I crossed the Charles River into Cambridge, Massachusetts. The only thing I knew about Cambridge was that Harvard and MIT were located there. Colleges meant kids, and kids meant fun was sure to be found.

Hospitality in Cambridge

What happened in Cambridge had a big impact on me. My ride dropped me off in the middle of the city, and I went into a sandwich shop to get something to eat. I bought a submarine sandwich and took it outside. There were no tables in front of the shop, but next door there was an apartment building with steps. I went to the steps, put my backpack down, and sat next to a fellow who was also eating a sandwich. We struck up a conversation. When we finished our sandwiches, he asked me if I wanted to stay at his apartment. He seemed like a nice guy, so I immediately accepted his offer.

We walked around the corner and up the stairs to his one-bedroom apartment. He told me he was leaving to stay with his girlfriend for a while. He said I could use the apartment while he was gone. We were about the same size, so he mentioned I was welcome to use his clothes as well. Before he left, he handed me the keys to his motorcycle and told me it was mine to use if I needed it. Finally, he gave me the address where he worked and asked me to drop off the keys to him when I left town. Then he was gone.

I was stunned by what had just happened. I had been in Cambridge less than one hour and was fully equipped. I had everything I needed, just like it had all been planned out in advance.

I walked through the apartment one more time. There was food in the refrigerator and some money left on top of his dresser. I slipped on a jacket from his closet; it fit me perfectly. I stared at the motorcycle keys. This was cool. I wished Larry Bresnan could see me now.

It was still not dark, so I decided to take a walk and find Harvard. In less than a mile I saw the ivy-covered brick buildings of the famous university. Students taking summer classes were walking from building to building, so I decided to act like I belonged at the school. I walked in the main entrance of a building and kept going up the stairs toward the second floor. I peered into a couple of empty classrooms and then headed back down the stairs. Halfway between the floors where the stairs turned, a girl was leaning against the wall. We smiled at each other. I stopped and asked her where she was from.

She was very friendly, and we kept talking. Eventually, I invited her over to the apartment and she accepted. At this point my story turns R rated, so I'll skip ahead. The next night we spent at her apartment. By the third day, our relationship had gotten too intense for me, and I wanted to get away from her.

I took the motorcycle and went for a ride through Lexington and Concord. I cruised down the roads once traveled by Paul Revere and the early patriots. Big leafy green trees formed canopies providing shade between the villages. It was a beautiful area for motorcycle riding and trying to forget someone back in Cambridge who wanted me to be in a committed relationship. I wanted to shake the guilt I was feeling.

I heard music in a town square when I returned to Cambridge. People were dancing and getting stoned, so I joined right in. I met a beautiful girl who was a good dancer. We had a great connection. I stayed with her for hours until she had to leave for work at a local drugstore.

The next day, I couldn't wait to be with this girl again. I went by the drugstore and found her. We got together when she got off work. We smoked marijuana together and our connection seemed magical. We walked around the city talking and laughing. We bought ice cream and kissed passionately.

It was one of the best days of my life, until it suddenly changed. We were sitting on a bench in a park when we were approached by an older Black guy who was dressed in leathers with dangling beads. They were friends. They were close friends. She was more interested in him than in me. After she pulled away from me, I headed back to the apartment with a heavy heart.

I decided it was time to leave Cambridge and head to Providence, Rhode Island.

I took the apartment and motorcycle keys to the job site of the guy who had given me access to everything he owned. I thanked him and began to hitchhike to Providence. My friend Bruce from high school had moved to Providence after our junior year. Before Andy and I left California, I had phoned Bruce and told him I hoped to visit him on our trip. I had written down his address and phone number, but I hadn't bothered to call him again. I assumed he would be home when I arrived.

Jail in Rhode Island

My ride to Rhode Island dropped me off in downtown Providence, the capital city of America's smallest state. I asked directions and walked a few blocks to Bruce's house. I heard bad news from his mother when she answered the door. Bruce had left on a surfing trip down the East Coast a few days earlier. She didn't expect him to return for a few weeks. Bruce had told her I might come by and she graciously invited me to stay with their family for a few days.

I called Andy that evening. We made plans for him to fly from San Francisco into Providence. We planned to visit a few places in New England before returning to New York City to pick up his van.

The night Andy flew into Providence did not go as planned.

I went with Bruce's sister and three other teenagers to pick up Andy at the airport. One of them, Tim, was engaged and having problems. Tim insisted we stop at a phone booth, so he could call his fiancée. I got out of the car with him because I didn't want him to take too long and make us late.

Within minutes, Tim was yelling into the phone. I began to feel sorry for the girl he was planning to marry. Suddenly, he screamed and slammed the phone down on the receiver. He then spun around and smashed his fist against the glass wall of the phone booth. The glass cracked like a giant spider web.

Two ladies were walking past us in the dark, just as Tim smashed the glass. As they both hurried away, one of them started screaming, "He broke the phone booth! He broke the phone booth!"

Tim emerged from the phone booth with his hand held high. Blood was dripping down his arm. He walked across the street to the Providence River and put his hand in the water to wash off the blood. He took off his shirt and used it to stop the bleeding and then got back in the car.

We rode in stunned silence as we resumed our drive to the airport. My thoughts were interrupted by a siren. Lights were flashing from a police car behind us. Our driver pulled over. Two policemen approached the car and ordered everyone out. We stood by the side of the road while the officers put Tim in handcuffs. They pushed him into the back seat of their patrol car and told the rest of us to follow them to the police station.

At the station, we were directed to a small waiting room and told to sit. After a few minutes, the officers returned. Tim was not with them. They asked each of us who we were and what we were doing when the phone booth window was broken. When it was my turn to speak, I told them I was visiting from California.

They eventually said we could go. When we all stood up to leave, one of the officers looked at me sternly and ordered, "Not you! Sit back down!"

I was shocked. Something was wrong, but I didn't know what. Once everyone else left, the cops had me stand up, empty my pockets, and take off my belt. They opened a door and led me into a large room lined with jail cells. We walked by a cell where Tim was lying down and seemed to be asleep. One officer opened a cell door on the far side of the room and stood next to it. The other one walking behind me made sure I kept walking until I was inside the cell. They shut and locked the door and walked out of the room. I grabbed the metal bars on the cell door. I had never been in a jail cell before. I felt like I was being framed in a bad movie.

I sat down to think. I knew I had a constitutional right to make a phone call, but nobody had given me a chance to make a call. I wanted to call Bruce's parents to tell them what had happened. Andy was at the airport. He didn't know where I was or why I wasn't picking him up.

After a while, the door into the cell area opened. A different officer came into the room carrying a broom. He began to sweep the floor. I stood up against the cell door with my hands around the bars. I wanted to talk to the officer, but I didn't want to be rude or make him angry. Trying to speak clearly and politely, I asked, "Sir, may I talk with you for a minute?"

He ignored me and kept sweeping. I waited a couple of minutes and spoke a little louder, "Sir, can I please speak with you for a minute?"

He kept sweeping with his head down. I didn't want to cause a scene, but I was feeling desperate. He picked up the broom and started walking toward the door to leave. My chance to make a phone call was slipping away. "Sir! Can I please make a phone call? I need to tell my friends where I am!"

He stopped, turned toward me and smirked. "You can't smash a phone booth in this city and get away with it!"

Then he walked out and shut the door. I couldn't believe it. I didn't smash the phone booth window. I was innocent. I'd been falsely accused, and they were not even giving me a phone call.

I sat back down on the bench. I had been worrying about Andy. Now I was worrying about myself. Would I ever get out of this jail? I could hear Tim sleeping deeply in the cell across the room. I concluded that he had been here before. After a while, I grew tired and sat down on a bench built into the cell wall. I couldn't rest; my mind was racing. I stared at initials and dates carved into the old wall by previous inmates. I was an all-American boy, but now I was in jail.

Several hours later, after midnight, the door to the room

opened again. An officer came to my cell and unlocked the door. I followed him as quietly and respectfully as possible back into the other room. He returned my belt, change, and wallet. He didn't say anything to me.

When I had everything back in my pockets, I decided to take a risk. "Sir, can you tell me why I was put in jail?"

"You were a suspicious person. We wanted to do a background check on you."

With that explanation, I was a free man and walked back to Bruce's house. Everyone was asleep when I arrived. I had no way to reach Andy, so I went to the bedroom and went to sleep.

The next day after breakfast, I joined Bruce's dad as he was watching the news. We saw policemen battling protesters in Chicago during the Democratic Convention. They were angry about the Vietnam War. I felt guilty that I wasn't with them joining in the protests.

While we were watching the demonstrations, Andy called. I was surprised when I realized he wasn't angry with me. Andy told me that while he waited for me, he had started talking to some girls at the airport. When I didn't show up, they invited him to join them in Provincetown, on the end of Cape Cod, where their parents had a vacation house. Later that day, I took a bus out to P-town to join them for the weekend.

It was a nice weekend exploring the town and partying with the girls. However, my desire for traveling had been more than satisfied. Andy phoned another friend from California, and they decided to continue the trip in the repaired van. I flew home to California.

PART TWO

DARK TIMES

CHAPTER FOUR

HOME AGAIN

W hen I returned home, I was excited to follow through on my plan to move out of Terra Linda and start attending the College of Marin. Larry Bresnan, Tim Yarish, and I moved into a two-bedroom house in Larkspur we rented for $150 a month. This was my first time living away from home.

Starting College

At the College of Marin, I tried to sign up for classes that required little work and allowed me to sleep in as late as possible. Most of the best classes were full, but I got on waiting lists. Since a lot of students were using marijuana and LSD, they were not showing up for classes as the days passed. I discovered if I simply stayed in the classes after the teachers said they were full, eventually students dropped out and there was room for me.

I took twenty-one units at College of Marin, but I didn't do much homework. Some of the classes, like history and public speaking, were easy for me to bluff my way through. In others, like physics, I started falling behind.

Partying

At our house in Larkspur, we had friends visit night and day to smoke marijuana and listen to music. This began causing me money problems. I was living on the money I had saved from delivering newspapers and working at Scotty's Market. I started dealing marijuana and hashish, so I could get stoned without blowing through all my money.

Every day was a party. It was a new concept to me and I liked it. I started getting high earlier each day. On weekends, we went to concerts or dances around Marin or in San Francisco. Almost everybody got stoned at the dances.

At a party in Tiburon, I met Sharman. We had a great time dancing together. I asked for her number. She laughed and said she knew I would never call her. I did call her. We began to go out together. She came to our house. Soon we were together almost every day. Sharman was smart and funny. I met her parents and her brother. They seemed to like me. They knew we dressed like hippies, but they didn't know we got stoned together every day.

A Really Bad "Trip"

As time went by, different friends brought their drugs over to our house to share. One day a guy brought over some MDA [synthetic mescaline]. He dissolved several large capsules into a cup, so three of us could each take some to get high.

I was selfish and greedy. I was the first to drink from the cup and I took more than my share. This time my selfishness came back to bite me. MDA creates a high similar to LSD. We thought it was safer since it mimics peyote, which is a plant, but we didn't understand its danger.

I was launched into a powerful psychedelic experience. I felt an intensity of focus that I had never experienced before. After eight hours when the high should have been wearing off, I was still as stoned as at the beginning. My friends started to come down that night, but my brain was so amped up I couldn't sleep. I was awake for the next three days.

By the second day, I felt like a supernatural power was working through me. It seemed like I was on a spiritual path. I thought I was getting revelations about the nature of life. I took a hike and saw stones on the ground that my hallucinating mind transformed into jewels. Common conversations with strangers seemed to contain deep hidden meanings with profound implications. Then I began to weep when I was talking to my friends. I didn't know what was happening or why I was crying. In my confusion, I went to the house of a psychologist to get some help. I thought I could tell what the psychologist was thinking before he spoke. He was troubled by our conversation, but he didn't give me any advice.

By the third day on this trip, I was weeping more frequently. I didn't feel sad, but I was coming unglued, like my heart was breaking. I thought the MDA was out of my system, and that I was a changed person with supernatural power. Strange thoughts entered my mind. I began to think I was an enlightened being who could save mankind. I imagined I was Jesus. I wanted to go on a mission to help people find the meaning of life.

I decided to find Sharman. I wanted her to go with me on my spiritual journey. I drove to the convalescent hospital where she was working. When I got there, I saw Sharman in the hallway, and told her to leave her job and come with me. She started crying. She realized something was wrong with me and explained she could not leave her job. One of her coworkers saw our confrontation and called 911.

I offered no resistance when two sheriff's deputies arrived and handcuffed me.

They took me to their station in downtown San Rafael for an interrogation. I felt like I was back in the principal's office in kindergarten, only this time the stakes were much higher.

After questioning me, the deputies decided to take me to Napa State Hospital. As we drove forty miles north, I remember thinking that Hitler was good and WWII was all wrong. A demonic spirit had gained access to my mind.

CHAPTER FIVE

NAPA STATE HOSPITAL

I was nineteen years old when my search for adventure and enlightenment landed me in a mental hospital. Napa State Hospital was home to more than 5,000 men and women in those days. Some had been locked up there for years; some would never leave alive. The psychiatric profession was even more experimental in 1969 than it is today, yet it was the best Northern California had to offer thousands of psychotic hippies and other mentally ill people.

We arrived at the hospital after dark, and I was put into Ward A-1, along with sixty other men.

I immediately recognized Vince playing pool in the ward's game room. We were both from Terra Linda, the suburb twenty miles north of San Francisco where I grew up. I told Vince I was going to get us out of the hospital that night. I had power and I would use it to free us. I rounded up some of the other patients and told them I was going to get them out as well.

Suddenly, several big men wearing white coats walked into the room, took my arms, and shoved me down the hall. I began to fight back but they pushed me into a small room. They jumped on me, pinning me to the floor. One of them took out a syringe and gave me a shot. They held me down until I passed out.

Thorazine Stupor

The next day I awoke in a small, padded, locked cell in Ward A-7. This ward was for catatonics who rocked back and forth without speaking and about fifteen of Napa's most disturbed patients. In addition to the individual locked rooms, the ward had a small common room with a television, a glass-walled room for the technicians, and a hallway.

On my first day, they brought breakfast to us on TV trays to the common room. One of the catatonics let out a screech and threw his tray on the floor. Two of the technicians in white coats yelled, grabbed him by each arm, dragged him back into his room, and locked the door.

I was willing to do or say almost anything to get out of Ward A-7. A few days later, I met with a psychiatrist and told him I was never going to do drugs again. I was going to go back to college. Furthermore, I was going to play football. I must have been persuasive. The next day, I was transferred back to A-1.

Confinement and Confusion

They didn't need a barbed-wire fence to keep me locked up. The Prolixin shot I received every week, along with my daily doses of Thorazine, kept me captive. If my daily dose of Artane was late, my hands shook like an old man with tremors. Artane was supposed to counterbalance the effects of the Prolixin. It confined me to the hospital better than thick brick walls ever could. When your mind is chained, your body has no way of escape.

I felt horrible. I thought I had ruined my life, and I deserved my fate. The psychedelic drugs I had taken had transformed me from a normal person into a confused, depressed demoniac.

As days went by in Napa, I felt trapped and remained confused. I began to think that since psychedelic drugs got me into this mess, maybe they could get me out of it. I wasn't aware my thinking was influenced by demonic forces that wanted to destroy me. I wanted to find a way to get my life back, and I became desperate enough to try anything.

One day, I saw something that made me question my situation. A new guy was brought into our ward. He was shouting wildly, claiming he was Jesus Christ. I knew right away that he was an imposter because I still thought I was Jesus. As days went by, I realized some of the wildest new arrivals were men claiming to be Jesus. Even though my MDA trip had been powerful, it was starting to occur to me that I might not be Jesus after all.

My parents came to visit me, and we had a meeting with a psychologist. During the meeting, I began to weep and started confessing sins from my past. I had been mean to my brothers. I had stolen newspapers from racks at the store and delivered them to my customers. I had been a liar. I had beaten up guys during fights at school.

At the time, my parents were on the verge of a divorce. I loved them both. I was ashamed I was a mental patient they had to visit in the hospital. I wanted to help them, but my predicament was making life more difficult for them.

Weekend Visits Home

After a few weeks, I was given a pass to go to my parents' house in Terra Linda for a weekend visit. Although I had been living with friends in Larkspur, the hospital would only release me to my parents' custody. My dad had moved out of the house, but was temporarily back home, along with my seven younger brothers and sisters.

The first night I returned home, Sharman came to visit me. She seemed distant and distressed by my confused condition. The medications I had been given made me shuffle and gave me a dazed stare. I was no longer the confident, party-loving boyfriend she had been dating.

On my second weekend home, Sharman told me that she had talked to my doctor and he had recommended we break up. I was shocked she would even consider listening to what the doctor advised. I loved her and thought she loved me as well. However, she took the doctor's advice and broke up with me that day.

I was devastated. For the first time in my life, I became suicidal. I went into my bedroom, which I shared with my three brothers. It smelled like a locker room because John, Barry, and Robert were playing football at Terra Linda High. My old shotgun was hanging on a rack on the wall. I thought about using it to end the agony of my depression.

As I considered suicide, thoughts of death and judgment scared me more than the pain of my depression. Still, I had no hope that someday things might get better. I believed my life had become a permanent mess.

Depression

I returned to the hospital at the end of each weekend visit. As much as I hated being locked up in a mental hospital, I didn't know what else to do, or where else I could go. I had no answers other than just trying to survive day by day. When you are feeling crazy, it is sometimes best to be in a place where everyone else feels crazy as well.

Some mornings after breakfast, I would go into the shower room at the hospital and sit on the floor letting the hot water beat down upon me. The comfort of the hot water hitting my head gave me a few minutes of relief from depression. One day, as I lay on the bed, I tried to remember a time when I enjoyed life.

I remembered a time in my childhood when my parents would take the family to the Russian River on summer vacation. Huge redwood trees lined the path to the river. My brothers and I went fishing and swimming. We played pinball machines at the river lodge. Back then, I experienced something that made life worth living. I wondered if it would ever be possible to have that feeling again.

I now understand that depression is accompanied by a false belief: Depressed people feel as if their life is irreparably broken and they will never feel normal again. They may know their depression was triggered by grief, a breakup, or a financial loss. Regardless of the cause, they believe the agony in their soul is permanent, and life will never be worth living.

After a few months, I briefly escaped from the hospital. I didn't run away, I simply walked out the main gate after being given the privilege to go outside on the lawn. I then hitchhiked to

Terra Linda. My mom was disturbed when I showed up unannounced because I was still delusional and angry.

After two days, my dad drove me back to Napa State Hospital. I was readmitted without fanfare. However, I entered with a new attitude. I was ready to take any medicine or try any treatment that might deliver me from depression and confusion.

Electroshock Treatments

Once inside the ward, I started kicking the wall and yelling that I wanted shock treatments. Electroconvulsive therapy [ECT] was given as a last resort to deeply depressed people. I didn't really know anything about ECT, or I would have never asked for it.

After my outburst, they put me back in Ward A-7. But after a few days, I was returned to Ward A-1 and scheduled for three electroshock treatments.

The next day, two technicians took me into a hospital exam room. They had me lie down on a table that had large straps. Next to the table was a black machine that looked like an electric guitar amplifier. The men cinched two straps tightly around my chest, pinning me to the table with my arms to my sides. A second pair of straps was used to hold my legs down.

When I asked what they were doing, they said they didn't want me to hurt myself during the treatment. That's when I got scared.

The technicians stepped away. The doctor attached wires with electrodes to my head. He put a piece of wood in my mouth that kept my tongue pressed down. I couldn't move or speak as he turned on the machine and adjusted the dials.

He then picked up a large syringe that looked like it should be used on a horse. He injected the needle into a vein in my arm and turned on a switch on the amplifier. I felt a current moving from the machine into my head. He began turning a dial on the machine, and the current grew increasingly stronger. My body started to squirm and writhe uncontrollably, like a giant hand was shaking my head. Suddenly, I couldn't breathe and started to panic. I frantically tried to take in air, but I couldn't get any oxygen. The spasms pulsating through my body increased in intensity. My body shook violently against the straps until the whole table shuddered. I felt like I was drowning and being electrocuted at the same time. Finally, I blacked out.

When I awoke, I was on the same table, but the straps had been released. I had a major headache, but I was glad to be alive. A nurse offered me two aspirin and I was led back to the ward.

It seemed funny to me that I was given all kinds of medication every day to treat my problems, but now that my head was really killing me from the ECT, my medicine was just two aspirin.

My immediate reaction to the treatment was that I didn't think anything had really changed. Several days later, I went through another electroshock treatment. It was as horrible as the first one. I was hoping it would somehow deliver me from the confusion I was feeling. It didn't.

In the end, the ECT experience only helped me in one significant way: I concluded that the mental health system at Napa State Hospital did not have the help I needed.

Doctor Gaw and Release from the Hospital

I was sure I would never get well in the hospital and became desperate to get out. I didn't want to be stuck there for years like some of the other patients I had met. I realized Dr. Gaw, the head psychiatrist for Ward A-1, was the key to my release. Based on his recommendation, patients were either sent home or hospitalized indefinitely.

One night, I saw Dr. Gaw working on charts at his desk inside the glass-walled cube at the end of our common room. I stood by his door and waited for him to acknowledge me so I could ask him when I would be released. I waited patiently, not wanting to cause any waves because he was a busy, powerful man. Dr. Gaw kept his head down, focusing on the charts. I knew he was aware of my presence on the other side of the glass wall, but he didn't acknowledge me.

Eventually, I decided to interrupt him. "Dr. Gaw, may I ask you a question, please?" He kept his head down, ignoring me.

I asked again a little louder, "Dr. Gaw, may I ask you a question please?" He still didn't respond.

I waited a couple of minutes, but my hope for a dialogue slowly faded. I walked away while contemplating my options. I knew that a sane person who is ignored when trying to ask someone an important question eventually gets angry. I wondered if Dr. Gaw was ignoring me to find out whether I was sane enough to get appropriately angry. Subsequently, I thought that maybe he wanted to keep me locked up in Napa for a long time, and if I got angry, he would then have an excuse to keep me in the hospital. I couldn't figure out the answer, but I walked back up to the glass wall and tried to talk with him again. I pleaded, "Dr. Gaw, may I please speak to you for a minute?"

No response, so I shouted, "Dr. Gaw, may I talk with you for a minute?!"

"Not now, Mr. Buckley!" he shouted right back.

Well, at least I knew he could hear me.

The next week, I had another encounter with Dr. Gaw. Again, I stood beside the glass wall and watched him work, hoping he would acknowledge me without a scene. But again, I was ignored. Eventually I shouted, "Dr. Gaw, may I please talk with you for a minute?"

To my surprise, Dr. Gaw looked up, just as if a normal person had asked him a routine question. He invited me to come in and sit down. "What is it, Mr. Buckley?" he asked when I took a seat next to his desk.

"Dr. Gaw, I am wondering if there is a chance that I will be released this week when you have your staff meetings and discuss my case."

He bent his head down to look at me over his reading glasses and asked, "Are you still hearing voices, Mr. Buckley?"

"What do you mean? I've never heard voices."

"Are you still hearing those voices, Mr. Buckley?"

"No, Dr. Gaw. I have never heard voices."

"That's all, Mr. Buckley."

"Dr. Gaw. I just want to know when I'm going to be released. I want to go home."

"That's all, Mr. Buckley!"

I walked away angry and upset, wondering if he was trying

to trap me. He had caught me off guard. I had never heard voices. Did he expect me to show him that I was a normal person and be very offended by the question? Or was he testing me to see if I had the patience I would need to be offended in the outside world and not react in anger?

I was released a few days later.

I had been in Napa State Hospital from late January until the beginning of June 1969.

CHAPTER SIX

STRUGGLING TO REGAIN MY LIFE

When I was released from the hospital, I moved back to my mother's house with my family in Terra Linda. I was still not well, and I knew it. I had been given a prescription of Thorazine to take at home. I hated Thorazine and couldn't wait to get off it, but I was afraid to quit taking it right away.

My mother provided a home where I could live without performance expectations until my soul healed. This was a gift from God. I needed to be around people who would let me be depressed without any condemnation.

I tried to reenter my former life, but without much success. One day, I went water-skiing with two high school friends. All I could do was sleep in the back of the boat in a Thorazine haze while they skied.

On another day, I sat in my bedroom taking a long look at my shotgun and thinking about suicide. If I shot myself it would be a bloody mess and I hated the sight of blood. I was scared by heights, so jumping off the Golden Gate Bridge did not appeal to me either. In my depressed state, I prayed, "God, if you get me out of this mess, I will become a priest." Based on the events that followed, I believe He heard me.

From then on, I discovered that something happened every day that made the day worth living. It might be as simple as someone smiling at me with a penetrating feeling of love, or someone picking me up hitchhiking and taking me right to my destination. Something good happened every day, and I realized it was no accident. I started wondering if God truly was calling me to become a priest.

Trying to Work

Jim Smith, our neighbor across the street, learned I needed work and hired me to work for a new company he had just purchased. I would be installing a protective window coating. I was cutting back on the medication I was taking, but any task that required coordination and effort for an entire day was more than I could handle. I was fired the second week after messing up the expensive coating several times.

It was the first of three jobs I would lose that summer.

My next job was as a diner cook. The other cook showed me how to put eggs, bacon, and hamburgers on the grill while the buns were toasting and the French fries were boiling, All the while new orders were coming in from the waitresses. The idea was that you flip the eggs and burgers, butter the toast, put sauce on the buns, add chicken to the grill for the new orders, pull out the fries, and make sure everything is perfect and finished on time. This is tough enough for a gifted person in his right mind. But believe me, no one taking Thorazine should ever attempt to cook four separate breakfast and lunch orders at the same time.

About an hour into the lunch run, I could sense that I was losing control of the situation. The restaurant was packed with diners, and orders were coming in from every waitress. I filled the large grill with burgers, bacon, eggs, and pancakes, but it was difficult for me to tell what needed to be flipped next. Then I heard a clear, strong voice. It didn't come from a person. It just was spoken into my mind, "This is not for you."

I realized I had just experienced one of the "voices" that Dr. Gaw had asked me about. Only crazy people are supposed to hear voices speak instructions into their minds. Yet, the voice I heard made a lot of sense to me.

It was obvious I had no business trying to be a cook when I was still under the influence of Thorazine. If the customers had known who was messing with their meals, they would have fled the restaurant. I quit the job that day and never received a paycheck.

My final job that summer was as a phone solicitor for a company that manufactured pool sweeps. Automatic pool cleaners are common today, but in 1969, they were so new that most people we phoned had no idea what we were trying to describe. I was confused enough as it was, so describing a floating thing with a long tail that managed to keep your pool clean and cost $1,000 was a big challenge.

I lasted a week and made no sales on the all-commission job. A highlight was when one of the other salesmen struck up a conversation with some girls on the phone and we arranged to go to Cupertino for the weekend to see them.

Surprisingly, amidst these failures, something important began to happen. My mind was clearing up and my sense of confidence and identity were returning.

Back to College and Drugs

In September I returned to College of Marin. I was now more cautious than I had been during my first semester. I initially resisted getting stoned. One of my most radical instructors ended up becoming a patient at Napa as well. I had smoked weed with him and another teacher at parties near the campus in Kentfield during my first semester. He used to teach that America was headed toward a revolution. The only revolution we experienced was the one that allowed our brains to be manipulated by demonic forces.

My mother's house was crowded with my seven younger siblings, and I was eager to move out. I saw an ad for a room to rent posted on a bulletin board at College of Marin. I called the phone number and soon moved into a rented three-bedroom house on Jessup Street in San Rafael.

My roommates were Jim and David. They both smoked weed. So, before long I was joining them. Eventually, I was smoking it several times a day. After a couple of months, I began to wake up every morning and throw up. This was the same reaction to marijuana I had experienced back in January, right before I had been committed to Napa. I realized it was making me sick, but I didn't want to give it up. I loved to get stoned and sit listening to music for hours every evening. That was what all my stoned friends enjoyed doing.

Betty Bethards, a spiritualist medium, was invited by our teacher to our communication class one day. Betty claimed she channeled spirits of people who had died. She had some powerful spirits speaking through her, but I was skeptical. She drank Pepsi and smoked continually between her channeling sessions. Even though I also smoked a pack of cigarettes a day, I thought spiritual people should be more at peace with themselves. I found myself evaluating the legitimacy of a doctrine by the impact the philosophy had on the teacher's personal life.

Haight-Ashbury

When school got out for spring break, I hitchhiked to Big Sur and camped on a beach for a couple of nights. It was fun to build big fires out of driftwood on the beaches to keep warm on foggy nights.

On the way back, I went through the Haight-Ashbury district of San Francisco. It was filled with people who looked spaced-out and lost. They had come from all over the country looking for love, yet many of them looked like they were a step away from being qualified for admittance to Napa State Hospital.

After walking around the city for several hours, I decided to spend that night in Golden Gate Park. I found a spot under some bushes on the edge of a big lawn in the park and went to sleep. Sometime in the middle of the night, I woke up wet. It seemed to be raining steadily, so I pulled my cloth sleeping bag over my head and went back to sleep.

I woke up as the sun came up. I poked my head out of my drenched sleeping bag and looked around. Water continued to cascade down on me, but it wasn't raining. I was sleeping under the sprinklers that were watering the park.

My Last "Trip"

I resumed going to concerts in San Francisco and getting stoned at all of them. Marijuana was passed from one person to another, depending on who you were standing next to at any given time. I sometimes took psychedelic drugs before I left home, because the effects would last up to eight hours.

One night, I took LSD with some friends before we went to Winterland to see Crosby, Stills & Nash. The concert was intense, with their voices blending in beautiful harmonies. We stayed, along with thousands of others, until the end. It was late that night before we got back to our house in San Rafael. My head was still buzzing from the LSD and I couldn't get to sleep.

I started to worry that I was on another trip I wasn't going to come down from, just like the one that had landed me in Napa. I wanted the stoned feeling to go away before I got into trouble. Jim wanted to keep the party going upstairs, but David was gone.

I still had a few Thorazine tablets left, so I decided to take some for the first time in months. Just to make sure it would work, I took a double dose and went downstairs to sleep in David's room in the basement.

David's bed was hanging by chains high up on the ceiling. He had a big metal wood-burning stove underneath that he would stand on to climb up to the bed. I climbed onto the steel stove, hoisted myself up onto the mattress, and soon fell into a deep Thorazine-induced sleep.

The next thing I knew, there was a loud clanging in the room. David's huge alarm clock was going off like a fire alarm. I sat up quickly and smashed my head on the ceiling. My brain was stunned from hitting the ceiling, as well as from a Thorazine hangover. I rolled over and lowered one foot to balance precariously onto the stove, then stretched my other leg down toward the floor.

Unfortunately, I didn't notice that the towering steel flue from the stove was beginning to fall. As I reached over to shut off the alarm clock, the flue fell like a sledgehammer onto my right big toe. Pain shot up my leg to my head. My head felt like a cartoon of the carnival game when the bell at the top rings after a guy with a sledgehammer pounds the plate at the bottom.

My toenail was smashed, my toe was bleeding, my brain was hungover. The situation was so ridiculous that I didn't even swear. I wiped the blood off of my smashed toe, and then climbed back up the lower portion of the stove onto the bed and fell back asleep.

I never took psychedelic drugs again.

PART THREE

SEARCHING FOR MY IDENTITY

CHAPTER SEVEN

QUEST FOR TRUTH

Visiting a Buddhist Monastery

One weekend early in the summer, I hitchhiked down the coast toward Big Sur. In my quest to find truth, I had heard about Tassajara, a Buddhist monastery in the mountains above Carmel Valley, and wanted to visit it.

I got a ride as far as the dirt road that led to the monastery, which was many miles up into the mountains. I waited in vain at the entrance to the road for a ride. No cars were coming, so I started walking up the road. After a few miles carrying my backpack, it seemed like the stones on the road were turning into jewels when I slowed down to stare at them. For the first time since I had gone to Napa, I was hallucinating, but this time it was without using drugs.

Eventually, an old pickup truck came up behind me, and the driver pulled over to give me a ride. We started talking right away. Wayne told me he was going to Tassajara. After driving several miles, he pulled over and we camped for the night. We slept on a ridge under the stars, watching shooting stars that looked like UFOs and talking about God.

The next morning, we completed the drive to the monastery

and were invited to join several monks and other guests as they went into a special room to meditate. Buddhist meditation is a practice of emptying your mind and focusing in ways that I never fully understood. I tried to use it to raise my consciousness, but it didn't bring me peace or insight.

Checking Out a Commune

I left Wayne at the monastery the next day and got a ride back down the mountain from another guest. Wayne invited me to visit him in Mendocino when I got the opportunity. He was living in a commune called "The Land." He didn't have a phone number and he didn't give me an exact address, but we both assumed I would have no problem finding him.

A couple weeks later I decided to hitchhike to Mendocino and take Wayne up on his offer. On the way there, I spent a night at a hippie commune outside Cloverdale. The hippies welcomed me with food and marijuana, but not having a girlfriend like the other guys made me feel lonely, so I headed back on the road early the next morning.

After arriving in Mendocino, I walked down one of the few residential streets, just as Wayne walked out of one of the houses— straight toward me. He just happened to be in town that day to finish a home repair job at the house from which he had just emerged. If we had had an appointment for that exact minute, we could not have timed our connection any better.

Wayne drove me up to The Land, which was twenty miles outside of town on Navarro Ridge. This was one of the events that helped me realize the first spiritual truth that ever stuck with me:

There is no such thing as an accident; everything happens for a purpose.

Little did I know how profoundly my understanding of that truth would be tested in the years to come.

Around thirty people were residing at The Land. The commune was owned by Sabina, a German lady, who had moved to America in search of a new life. She bought acreage on Navarro Ridge and opened The Land to anyone who wanted to come and build a home among the pine and fir trees.

Sabina lived in her own large wood house. Another house was used by the entire commune as a communal kitchen and living room. They shared a common garden on the open space on top of the ridge. Several men were also building smaller houses out of whatever wood they could buy, mill, or find.

I spent the night with Wayne and his girlfriend in a house they had built on a hillside on the far edge of the commune. They left on a trip the next day and told me I was welcome to use their house for as long as I liked.

I stayed a few days. The people at The Land intrigued me. I liked their friendliness and the idea of everyone sharing resources. I heard that they needed to put in a new water system for their garden and thought about emptying my bank account to help them. In the end, I decided not to. Rather than give the commune my last two thousand dollars, I would take the trip to Europe Larry Bresnan and I had planned to take after high school. After that, perhaps I would return and settle down on The Land.

This experience led me to start exploring different approaches to God. I knew God had helped me get out of depression, and in the back of my mind, I remembered my promise to become a priest. I had seen enough supernatural things to know God was real, but I wasn't sure how to connect with him.

So, when I returned to Marin, I tried to take truth from many sources. I was drawn toward healing, so I started going to Christian Science meetings and reading the book by their founder, Mary Baker Eddy, *Science and Health with Key to the Scriptures*. I also attended a metaphysical church in Marin and occasional Bahia meetings. I met some nice people in these groups, but I did not feel a real connection with any of them.

Breakthrough in Los Angeles

Larry Bresnan and I got back together as I struggled through the summer. One day he suggested we take a trip to Los Angeles. I agreed, and it changed my life.

Unlike our other trips, we didn't hitchhike on this one. This time, Larry drove.

In Los Angeles, we connected with a group of Christians who were unlike any people I had ever been around. They read the Bible, quoted scriptures, and talked about God constantly. Larry and I went to one of their meetings. One person after another stood up and read a passage from the Bible. This intrigued me. I had heard scriptures read in the Catholic Masses as a boy, but I had never read the Bible myself.

We spent two nights with one of the families in the group. I was touched by how they treated us with love and respect.

The first night we stayed with this family, I had a powerful dream: I saw Jesus walking along a path with several of His disciples. He stopped and pointed to the sky. Light from heaven was filtering through the clouds. The light was glorious and alive. The power of the Spirit emanated from heaven's light. Jesus drew us closer to the brilliant light, until we crossed into heaven itself. My dream then entered a second stage. In this phase of the dream, I was playing pool and making all my shots. Then I was bowling, throwing one strike after another. I loved competition, and this part of the dream had me competing nonstop and winning every contest.

I woke up. I had never felt like this before. Peace from the light of heaven had filled my heart. And, for the first time in more than a year, I felt no desire to have a cigarette that morning.

As I contemplated the dream, I knew that Jesus had revealed the glory of the light of heaven to me. I also realized that the heaven I saw in the second phase of my dream was not the heaven where God's presence dwelt. It was the heaven I was trying to create for myself through my love of competition. Even though in the dream I played with a competence I had never experienced before, my idea of heaven was nothing compared to the glory Jesus had allowed me to see.

Is Jesus Really Alive?

After we returned from Los Angeles, I lost track of Larry for a couple of months. In December, he came to visit me and moved into our San Rafael rental house for a month. Larry had changed. He was now reading the Bible every day and talking about Jesus all the time. Two of his friends were also following the Lord, and he brought them over to our house. They told me they didn't need to smoke weed anymore because they had joy from the Lord. They called each other "brother" and seemed to really like each other. It was easy to discern that they had something going for them that I didn't have.

I tried to show them hospitality, but I wasn't ready to take the step of asking Jesus to be my Lord, as they were encouraging me to do. I wondered, in fact, just how committed they were to what they were telling me.

One night, as a test, I offered them some wine. I wanted to see if their message was the same when they had a few glasses of wine, as it was when they were sober. Larry had one glass of wine and wouldn't accept another. The other guys only drank tea. Their message and their lifestyles were consistent.

I liked what they had. But their message about Jesus Christ being "the way, the truth and the life," and the only way to the Father, seemed too narrow for me. I also knew Larry had not only quit smoking marijuana, but he was also staying celibate. I didn't know if I could spend the rest of my life without smoking weed. And if I did accept Christ, I sure didn't think I could stay celibate until marriage. Those seemed like huge commitments to me.

At the end of December, Larry moved out and headed to Oregon.

I kept thinking about what he told me before he left. "Just ask Jesus Christ to come into your heart and be your Lord and Savior." Ever since I was a child, I had believed that Jesus Christ was the Son of God and that he died on the cross and rose from the dead. The Catholic Church had taught me those truths. We said the Apostle's Creed at every Mass, and I believed it.

However, I knew there was a big difference between Larry's life and mine. He was living as if he really believed that Jesus Christ was alive. I was living to have as much pleasure as possible every day and hoping that God would understand and accept me if there really was going to be a day of judgment.

As a young boy riding my bicycle around Terra Linda, I would occasionally stop at St. Isabella's Catholic Church and pray. I wanted to make sure, in case there was a hell, I wouldn't be going there. Jesus had always intrigued me. He was the one who healed the sick. He was the one who died for our sins. He was the one who gave His life for me, even though I did nothing to earn His love.

Larry's message seemed narrow to me, but if Jesus was alive, I did want to meet Him.

So, after a few weeks of thinking about it, one night alone in bed, I prayed just as Larry had told me to pray: "Jesus, I believe you died on the cross for my sins. Please forgive my sins. Please come into my heart and be my Lord and Savior." Nothing very dramatic seemed to take place, but I felt peace after praying this prayer. I was no longer running away from the Lord. I was going to give Him a chance and see what happened.

If you have never given your life to Jesus, I would like to encourage you to pray that simple prayer as well.

At the time, I didn't think I was risking too much with the prayer because I thought I could always go back to my old lifestyle. Yet, somehow in my heart, I felt things were going to be different. I had no idea how very different my life was going to become.

CHAPTER EIGHT

STARTING A NEW LIFE

As 1970 began, I lived on Jessup Street in San Rafael, attended College of Marin, worked as a janitor at the recreation center in Terra Linda, and played on the college tennis team.

First Time Reading a Bible

I found an old King James Bible in the house and randomly opened it to read the Bible for the first time in my life. I found myself reading Ecclesiastes 3:

> To everything there is a season, and a time to every purpose under the heaven: A time to be born, and a time to die; a time to plant, and a time to pluck up that which is planted; A time to kill, and a time to heal; a time to break down, and a time to build up; A time to weep, and a time to laugh; a time to mourn, and a time to dance.

I recognized the words from a song by The Byrds. Was this my time? Was this a message to me? I continued to read and felt overwhelmed by the depth of the words.

In the following days, I often opened the Bible randomly, but I soon realized that much of it was difficult to understand. So, I tried a different approach. Since the words of Jesus in the Bible were printed in red, I started focusing on those words as I read through the Gospels. I found most of the words of Jesus were simple, yet profound.

My Schedule

After I was released from Napa Hospital, my driver's license was suspended for a year. When I received the notification from the DMV, I assumed it was because I had gotten too many traffic tickets in the past. At one time or another, I got tickets for almost every conceivable offense: speeding, going the wrong way on a one-way street, abandoning a vehicle containing marijuana, etc. Later, I learned that many mental patients had their licenses suspended due to the medications they were taking.

I hitchhiked every morning from San Rafael to Kentfield for classes. Around noon, I finished my classes, and hitchhiked from Kentfield to the recreation center in Terra Linda. Then after working for two hours, I hitchhiked from Terra Linda back to Kentfield to make tennis practice by 3:00 P.M. There were no direct routes from Kentfield to Terra Linda and back. Every trip took two or three rides to get to my destination. I didn't have much time between the end of classes and the start of work, or the end of work and the start of tennis practice or matches. Yet every single day, without fail, I was on time for school, work, and practice.

I began to believe that this was not an accident. It couldn't be an accident; there had to be something supernatural going on. For some reason, God was watching over me and providing for me. Somehow, the Lord made sure that each day I got to where I needed to be going.

One day it took longer than usual to get my rides. I was running late for work when I was dropped off at the entrance to Terra Linda. I was still a mile away from the recreation center. I started walking along the side of the road with my left arm extended and my thumb pointed up. A shiny, black sports car pulled over to give me a ride. I got into the car of a well-dressed man a few years older than me.

I was only with him for a few minutes as he took me to the recreation center. I wanted to talk with him about the Lord, but I was afraid he would say, "If I accept Jesus, will I end up like you? You look like a penniless kid with no car, hitchhiking to work. Why would I want to trade my life for yours?"

In the end I did say something to him about Jesus. It occurred to me that no matter now nice a man's car and clothes, if he doesn't know Jesus, he does not know the real meaning and purpose of life. I had begun to believe, no matter how cool a guy may look, he is nothing compared to the Man who can heal the sick, forgive our sins, and send us the Holy Spirit.

After two months of these divine coincidences, I began to get headaches every day. I had never had a headache that lasted for more than an hour in my life. I never took aspirin before this. Now I was getting migraines that made my head feel like it was being pierced by a spike.

After a few weeks of migraines, I decided God was trying to give me a message. I realized I was living the life of a hypocrite. I believed in the Lord and was reading the Bible, but I was still smoking marijuana every day and looking for girls to pick up. I felt God was watching over me, but I was not living the life I was supposed to be living.

Lessons from a Skiing Trip

Although I had no driver's license, I still occasionally drove my brother Barry's car. One afternoon in San Rafael, I was pulled over for speeding in Barry's car. Since I didn't have a license to show the officer, I put Barry's name and address on the ticket. I felt badly about it, but I rationalized that he owed me for the times he used to sneak my MGB out at night and bring it back with dents. Barry wasn't happy when he had to go to court and pay the fine, but he paid the ticket without turning me in.

One winter day, I decided to go skiing with a girl I was dating and my friend Mike. I had no license, but I was driving her car. As we drove into the mountains toward Lake Tahoe, I stopped and picked up a hitchhiker. The snow was deep along the highway because a big snowstorm had hit the Sierras that week. Only one lane was open on I-80 in each direction, and the snowplows had created huge banks of snow on either side of the lane. I drove slowly because we didn't have snow chains.

As we approached the crest of the mountain, I looked up into the rear-view mirror and spoke to the hitchhiker, "Just between you and me and the Lord up above . . ." Then I looked down from the mirror to the road in front of me. About a hundred yards ahead, the only lane of the highway was blocked by a car that had spun out and was stuck in the snow bank. The car door was open, and a lady had one foot in the car and her other foot on the road.

I immediately hit the brakes. My car started to skid down the icy highway. The lady froze. She didn't move an inch as we skidded toward her. In what seemed like slow motion, we barely missed her and rammed into her car. She screamed as we made impact near her front headlight. Fortunately, no one was hurt.

In hindsight, I should have hit my brakes more lightly. I also should have tried to steer into the snow bank to avoid the collision. Clearly, I froze, as the lady had. I didn't know what I was going to tell the highway patrol officer who was sure to come soon. I couldn't put this one on Barry. When the officer came, I put my name on the ticket.

My Godfather's Influence

Our car was too damaged to drive, so we called a tow truck. We got a ride into Tahoe City, where my godfather, Owen Sullivan, had a house owned by his company. Since I knew where the key to the house was hidden, I figured we could stay there. I didn't call and ask Owen's permission; in my narcissistic mind, I was sure it would all work out in the end.

Owen had always shown interest in me as I grew up. Every Christmas I received a card, along with a subscription to *Sports Illustrated*, from Owen and his wife, Gloria. The card always contained a letter with the question, "How are your faith and morals?" At the time, I didn't know what "faith and morals" meant. I assumed they went together, but I really didn't know what Owen was referring to, other than that faith and morals had something to do with God.

The next morning, I called Owen to tell him we were in his house in Tahoe. I was motivated to call by the fact that we were now stuck in the house with no way to get to the ski slopes.

Owen was upset we had not asked his permission to use the house. So that afternoon, he and Gloria made a hasty four-hour drive from Walnut Creek to Tahoe. When they arrived, he gave me a stern warning not do it again; then, he calmed down. He had twin daughters who were pretty obedient, and deep down he seemed to enjoy the adventures of his godson.

Words of Wisdom

Two more things happened that weekend that have stayed with me through the years.

First, I told Owen about the promise I had made to God when I was very depressed.

"I told God that I would become a priest if he got me through the depression I felt after leaving Napa," I explained. "But I don't know if I can handle the celibacy part of the Catholic priesthood. I would really like to get married someday."

"Why don't you become an Episcopal priest?" Owen asked. "They can be married."

I was shocked to hear my faithful Catholic godfather suggest such a thing, yet his reply opened my mind to the possibility that I could fulfill my promise to the Lord to be a priest . . . and have a family at the same time. A few years later, I discovered the New Testament teaching that all Christians are called to be "a kingdom of priests" (Revelation 1:6).

I'm very thankful the Lord had a bigger understanding of

priests than my limited knowledge when I made the promise.

The next day, the car was repaired enough to drive, so Mike and my girlfriend decided to go back to Marin. I stayed and went skiing with Owen. After our day on the slopes, Owen started driving Gloria and me home. I was exhausted and lay down on the back seat of the car to rest.

We headed out Highway 89 along the Truckee River toward I-80. Owen was usually a responsible driver, but not on this cold winter night. He was driving about sixty miles an hour down a highway with steep snow banks on our right and a lane of traffic next to the iced-over Truckee River on our left.

Soon after I lay down on the back seat, we hit a patch of black ice on the road. The car went into a 360-degree spin. As I felt the car go into the spin, all I could say was "Jesus." I thought we might die, so I put myself in the hands of the Lord. The car spun across the other lane toward the river and smashed into a pile of snow. We landed with a big thud. Owen hit his head on the steering wheel, and I was thrown off the back seat, but Gloria and I were fine.

We got out of the car and saw the front left tire and headlight buried in the snow pile. We were able to dig it out and push the crushed bumper away from the tire so that we could continue to drive. Owen drove home a lot slower, with each of us contemplating the reality that our lives were just spared. Owen told me later that as he drove home, a part of him wanted to kill me for getting him into this mess and another part of him was just thankful to be alive.

About a month after the accident, I received a summons to appear in a court near Lake Tahoe. My dad drove me to the courthouse from Terra Linda. Throughout the three-hour drive, he never uttered a word of rebuke about my foolish behavior. He might have figured that his own sins were worse than mine and the punishment of the court would be enough to teach me a lesson.

The judge fined me $100 for getting into an accident with a suspended license. I knew I had two strikes against me, so I started hitchhiking exclusively and planned to wait a year before reapplying for a driver's license.

CHAPTER NINE

GROWING CLOSER
TO GOD

Telling Others about Jesus

One evening, as I hitchhiked home, a man picked me up and gave me a ride to the house on Jessup Street. I was trying to be friendly by asking him some questions about his life, as I always did when someone gave me a ride. As we talked, I realized he was having problems. I got the feeling I should tell him about Jesus. However, I wasn't sure how to start that conversation.

As we reached my house, I decided to just plunge into it. I don't remember anything I said, but I do remember what happened. As soon as I started talking about Jesus, words came into my mind that made sense. A message started to flow out of me like water flowing down a stream. One sentence led to the next. I remembered things from the New Testament I had been reading that I did not know were in my heart until that very moment. I talked, and he listened for the next five or ten minutes, and then he drove away.

I walked into the house and sat down to think about what had happened. I knew I wasn't that smart—especially about spiritual things. Yet, the Lord had given me words to say beyond my understanding. I remembered what Jesus had said about the Spirit:

If ye love me, keep my commandments. And I will pray the Father, and he will give you another Comforter, that he may abide with you for ever; Even the Spirit of truth; . . . (John 14:15–17 [KJV]).

I realized the Spirit of truth had been speaking through me. I understood that the Comforter whom Jesus had been talking about was within me. For the first time in my life, I was certain Jesus had risen from the dead because He had sent me the Spirit. I was excited. I wanted to get closer to the Lord and tell others that Jesus is alive.

Putting His Words into Practice

After that encounter, I started reading the New Testament every evening. I would start reading a chapter and within those verses it seemed like there was a message just for me. Sometimes the message was about forgiveness; other times it was about love, serving, or giving.

I realized I had been a self-centered man, and that I had been greedy all my life. The words of Jesus challenged me. I decided to try an experiment. I would attempt to put the message I received from the Bible into practice every day. If Jesus said to give, I found someone to give to. If He said to serve, I would do the dishes or clean the house to serve my roommates.

Putting the words of Jesus into practice began to have a profound impact on me.

One day, I read in 1 Corinthians 6:19 that our bodies are temples of the Holy Spirit. I had been smoking a pack of Marlboros every day since I had gone to Napa, and I knew I should quit. I asked God to help, but it was still a struggle.

After a few failed attempts to quit cold turkey, I came up with a plan. Every day I tried to have my first cigarette a little later in the day. First, a little later in the morning, then later in the afternoon, and eventually after dinner, when I usually sat at the table and enjoyed a cigarette. Ultimately, instead of sitting at the dinner table and smoking, I moved into the living room and opened my Bible to read. The words of the Bible brought me peace and took my mind off smoking a little longer. I started taking walks after my Bible-reading time. Within a few weeks I had smoked my last cigarette.

Attending My First Bible Study

In those days, I kept half a cardboard refrigerator box in my bedroom for my dirty laundry. When I started running out of clean clothes, I rummaged through the box until I found socks or whatever I needed that weren't quite as dirty as my other options. About once a month, I was forced to drag the box of dirty clothes down the street to the laundromat.

One washday, I sat next to a guy who was reading a book called *Good News for Modern Man*. I asked him about the book. He told me it was a modern New Testament. He was attending a Bible study right down the street in San Anselmo on Tuesday nights. He invited me to come sometime.

The next Tuesday night, I went to the first Bible study of my life.

The house was packed with guys who had long hair and girls who looked like they were going to a rock concert. I found a place on the floor and listened as a young man named Ken Sanders, with black hair and dark skin, played a guitar and led them in songs. Between songs, different people read scriptures from the Bible and talked about what Jesus had done for them. They had the same kind of love I had seen in Los Angeles with Larry the year before, but these people were more like me.

At the end of the meeting, I was waiting in line to use the bathroom when I noticed a barefoot girl with long brown hair and hazel eyes. Her complexion was clear, and her figure would qualify her for a men's magazine. I was intrigued by her smile and hoped to get to know her better. I found out her name was Kristina. I had no sense she would one day be the most important person in my life.

Resisting Temptation

Over the next few months, I was trying to figure out God's love and understand His ways, but I was still intrigued by other spirits. For example: My grandmother Mathews had given me a signet ring that had belonged to her mother, Beatrice, who had been a spiritualist medium. The ring was gold with the face of Jesus carved on a precious stone inlaid in the gold. Grandma knew I was trying to follow Jesus, and she explained that her mother considered the ring very powerful. The ring fascinated me because of its association with the occult and spiritual power. The idea that spirits had power and knowledge made me hunger for more spiritual truth.

I soon had an opportunity to test the power of the ring.

In May, I took a trout-fishing trip with Jim Walker and one of his friends. We drove to Oregon where we camped and fished for three days. I considered myself a good trout fisherman, but compared to these guys, I was a novice. Each day, I caught a couple of trout, while my friends caught more than twenty.

On our drive back to Marin, I forgot my disappointment in my fishing ability when we made a detour to do some gambling in Reno. I had spent a lot of time playing poker and blackjack with friends in high school, but I had never gambled in a casino. The three of us were a year short of the legal gambling age of twenty-one, but they knew a casino where nobody would check our IDs.

We drove into Reno and found the casino. My heart was pounding as we walked into the smoky gaming room lit by rows of slot machines. When I sat down at the blackjack table, I pulled the Jesus signet ring out of my pocket, rubbed its face, and asked God to give me the power to win.

Over the next hour I experienced something that changed my life. I began to get a distinct sense about whether I would win or lose the hand of blackjack before the cards were dealt. I began to experiment by putting up one or two dollars when I had a bad feeling about the upcoming hand. Then I would increase the bet to five dollars if I had a good feeling. Time after time, the premonition was accurate.

By the end of an hour, I had a big stack of chips in front of me. However, I also had the feeling that a powerful spiritual force was working to draw me into gambling. I realized that all I had to do was to listen to this spirit and I could make a lot of money gambling. At that moment I began to feel that the spirit drawing me into gambling was actually from the devil.

I got up from the table and walked outside the casino.

My mind was racing as a battle between good and evil raged within me.

If there is a devil, then there must be a God as well. If God is real, why would I want to waste my time playing blackjack? If I make it my priority to get to know God and serve Him, then He will take care of me.

I walked from the casino parking lot to the bank of the Truckee River. I took the signet ring out of my pocket and stared at the face of Jesus on the ring. I prayed out loud, "God, I believe you are real, and you can take care of me. You can give me all the money I'll ever need. I don't want to waste my time. I don't want to serve the devil. I want to serve you."

I pulled my arm back and threw the ring into the Truckee River. The river was flowing quickly and it was too dark to see it splash. I was sorry to throw such a beautiful ring into the water, but I was excited to discover what my life would be like when I started seeking God with the same passion I had once used to seek money. I felt in my heart I had a deal with the Lord. If I would serve Him, He would take care of me financially.

My confidence in that "deal" would be tested in many ways in the years ahead. But God has remained faithful. At times I had to sell a few things to pay my bills, but I have had all the money I have really needed for our family and our ministry.

I went back into the casino, cashed in my chips, and announced that I was ready to leave. My friends were ready to go as well. They had lost all the money they wanted to lose.

CHAPTER TEN

TIME TO TRAVEL AGAIN

One weekend afternoon after the trout-fishing trip, I hitchhiked up Mount Tamalpais, the highest point in Marin County. I had come to the mountaintop many times to look west at the sun setting into the Pacific Ocean. On this trip while at the top of the mountain, I turned to the east. As I gazed into the distance, I thought about what a big country America is and how many people live east of California. I thought about the trip to Europe Larry and I had planned and then canceled after our high school graduation. I decided it was time to put our traveling plan into action. I would leave as soon as the college semester ended in June. I wasn't sure how far I would go, but this time I would travel alone.

At the end of May, I moved out of the Jessup Street house and brought my clothes to my mom's house. When I told mom about my plans to hitchhike across the country and fly to Europe, she looked sad and asked me to be very careful. She could have used my help with my seven younger brothers and sisters. But I believed I had to figure out what I was doing in this world before I could really help her—or anyone else.

I stopped by the rental car company where my dad was

working and told him about my travel plans. He could tell that I was excited and nervous about the trip. He encouraged me and then declared, "The Irish should not die apart from Ireland." His words did not give me much comfort because I was hoping not to die, and I had no plans to visit Ireland.

In the middle of June, I packed my clothes along with a copy of *Good News for Modern Man* into my backpack and tied my sleeping bag to its top. I walked down Freitas Parkway to the on-ramp where I had hitchhiked many times before. This time, however, I was heading east, knowing there was a big country to explore and a lot of miles to cover.

I had several hundred dollars in traveler's checks and a promise from my mom that she would wire me money from my bank account if I ran low. The money I had made delivering newspapers and working at Scotty's Market was now going to be invested in an adventure, which I hoped would help me discover the meaning of life and my place in it.

Adventures across America

For a month I hitchhiked across the United States with many stops along the way.

A Fish Story

I spent one night at a state park campground in Illinois. After dropping off my backpack at a campsite where several young people had tents, I went exploring and found a meandering river. Two young boys were fishing on the riverbank. As I watched them staring at their poles, I imagined Jesus standing on the shore of the Sea of Galilee. At that time, I still had lingering delusions about being

Jesus. What happened next did not end my confusion.

There was a nearby spot where the river made a turn next to a fallen tree. I could sense that would be a good place to fish. I walked up behind the boys. They turned to look at me as I approached.

"Have you guys caught anything?"

"Nope. Nothing."

"Cast your lines over there," I suggested in my deepest voice, pointing to the partially submerged tree. Then, I walked back to the campsite to make sure my backpack was still secure. Everything was fine at the campsite. A couple of new people had arrived. I was getting to know them for a few minutes when I heard a small voice behind me.

"Mister! Mister!"

I turned to see the two boys who had been fishing. One of them was carrying their two poles. The other had his arms extended toward me—with two big bass.

"We caught them right where you told us to," the boy declared, as he dropped the bass at my feet.

I was as shocked as the boys were. Each bass was three or four pounds. The boys had probably never caught fish that big in their lives. Outwardly, I acted like it was no big deal, but inwardly, I wondered if I had the power of Christ and should launch into a new dimension of ministry. I told them to keep the fish, which they picked up as they walked away.

The next day my travels got more bizarre.

Creepy Companions

I started hitchhiking north on Highway 41 through Illinois.

The first car to stop had two friendly, clean-cut guys in the front seat. They were headed to Chicago. I had never been to Chicago, so I told them I would love to go with them. We had a good talk for the first hour or two, but then they both became quiet. As we continued the long drive, the guys became agitated. They were both itching and scratching as they grew more upset. Their behavior didn't make sense to me at the time.

It was dark by the time we entered the suburbs of Chicago. If it had been daytime, I would have had the guys drop me off, because they were no longer friendly. We continued toward the inner city, which was dark, foreboding, and humid. We arrived at a huge high-rise apartment complex, and they both began to talk excitedly. I was uncomfortable, but I figured I would be better off with them than taking my chances on the streets of Chicago at night.

The guys told me I could crash for the night in their friend's apartment. We took the elevator up twenty floors and walked down the hall, where they knocked on a door. A friendly guy with short hair answered the door and welcomed us in. I began to relax when we walked into this big apartment. It had nice sofas and a view of the city lights below.

The host offered us tea, but the men were there for something else. They told our host they needed some stuff right away. He smiled and walked into another room. When he reappeared, he had a little toolbox with him. He sat down, opened the box, took out a syringe, and started to attach a needle to it.

The men started talking excitedly like they were about to open Christmas presents. One by one, they rolled up their sleeves, took large rubber straps, and wrapped them around their forearms, making tourniquets. It took a few minutes before I realized what was happening. Watching them was fascinating and repulsive at the same time. I had never seen anyone shoot up heroin before.

My formerly agitated friends became mellow after their injections. They came over and started talking to me, with the same smiles they had when they picked me up that afternoon. I realized these clean-cut guys were heroin addicts.

The man who lived in the apartment told me he was a social worker. He had a job that paid him to help people straighten out their lives, yet he was a junkie. By the time he was being injected by the driver of our car, I told them all I had to get going. I did not know where I would go, but the dark streets of Chicago seemed safer to me than sharing an apartment with men shooting heroin.

Scary Surroundings

It was near midnight when I descended in the elevator and walked out of the high rise into the muggy night. A nearby parking lot contained a few old cars that were waiting like faithful horses for men at a late-night bar. Scraggly bushes lined the lot. I looked up and down the street for a better option, and then went into the bushes and unrolled my sleeping bag. I had slept in strange places, but this was my first time sleeping in parking lot bushes.

I woke up in the bushes early the next morning, rolled up my sleeping bag, attached it to the backpack, and started walking. The neighborhood looked worse in the daylight than it had the night before. Trash littered the sidewalks and the streets. As I walked past old brick buildings, Black men emerged from the shadows, staring at me as though I was a foreigner who had invaded their territory. They had probably been up all night.

I realized I was in a black ghetto on the south side of Chicago. I found a fast food place for breakfast and then, following directions from strangers, started walking toward the nearest freeway. I walked a long way, avoiding eye contact with a few hostile-looking men on the street, and finally hitched a ride over the state line into Gary, Indiana.

Church in Gary, Indiana

Though Gary was hardly paradise, I was relieved to be out of Chicago. I saw people walking into a Lutheran church for Sunday morning services, so I followed them and set my backpack on the pew next to an older couple. The hat-wearing lady looked at me with disdain when I received communion. I didn't know what their communion policy was, but I was thankful to be alive and wanted to draw closer to Jesus by receiving communion. I figured she would get over her indignation that a smelly, backpack-toting stranger thought he was qualified to receive the body and blood of Christ.

Close Call in Ohio

After the service, I walked to a freeway on-ramp and continued east. The next day, somewhere in Northern Ohio, my trip almost got derailed.

I was dropped off at a diner around lunchtime and went inside to get something to eat. I saw several guys playing pool. I liked shooting pool and considered myself pretty good at it. During high school, my friend Bill Saleme and I would often shoot pool after football practice. We usually played for a couple of dollars a game and came out fairly even. If I was behind and we had come in my car, no matter how late it got, Bill was not going to get a ride home unless we played "double or nothing", until I won my money back.

Playing with Strangers Can Be an Entirely Different Game

The guys at the table were good pool players playing nine-ball for five dollars a game. I wanted to play, because I like camaraderie and competition. I also thought I could beat the guy who was winning.

He beat me the first game. We played "double or nothing" on the next game. I lost that game and we doubled the bet again. I should have won those double-or-nothing games, but he won them both, after my cue ball was out of position at the end of both games. I then got nervous and lost a fourth straight game.

I was seething as I walked away from the table. I was on a tight budget, and if I was going to keep this trip going through the summer, I couldn't afford to lose forty dollars playing pool. Worse yet, I felt like the guys were snickering at me when they resumed playing.

Then the moment of truth came. I walked back to the table and told the guy who beat me that I wanted to go double or nothing one last time for the forty dollars I had lost to him. He immediately took me up on the offer, racked the balls, broke, and started shooting better than ever. He almost ran the table and had a clear shot at the nine-ball to win the game.

I was sweating, and my heart was pounding while he chalked up his cue stick for one last shot. I figured I would have to start heading back to California if he made the shot. He missed the shot but left me a difficult bank shot on the nine-ball. I recited a quick, intense prayer: "Lord, please forgive me for trying to get revenge. Please help me and I'll never do this again." I lined up the bank shot. It was a shot I would make about 30 percent of the time. My heart was pounding as I struck the cue ball.

Then I saw something I had never seen before or haven't seen since. The nine-ball hit the rail and seemed to curve as it went into the opposite side pocket. I was stunned, and the other guys were aghast. I won all my money back on a shot that should not have gone into the pocket.

I collected my money. My opponent immediately asked for a rematch, which I declined. I felt very light as I walked out of the diner. I had received a minor miracle from the Lord that had saved my trip. I was determined to remember this lesson and never seek revenge again.

On to Pennsylvania

The next day, a friendly man picked me up and drove me to the outskirts of Indiana, Pennsylvania. We talked about the Lord on the drive before he dropped me off in front of a small evangelical church. As he drove away, I felt drawn to go inside the church. I saw several copies of *Good News for Modern Man* sitting on a table in the foyer. I stayed long enough to pray and then began a long walk through the city.

I stopped at the university campus, where students my age were heading to summer classes. There were a lot of green trees and it looked like a great place to go to school. I continued walking down the tree-lined streets to a bus stop. When the bus came, I got on board and rode it to the far end of town and started hitchhiking again. Then a thought came to me, "This is a beautiful city. Where am I going in such a hurry that is any better than here?"

I turned around and walked back into town. Shortly thereafter, I met John Varner, who was a middle-class, family man about ten years older than me. He and his wife attended a traditional church in the city, and they were hungry for a deeper relationship with God. John was impressed that I loved Christ and was traveling around the country trying to learn more about the Lord. I think he mistook my searching for humility and wisdom.

John's Hospitality

John provided me a place to stay in a house he was fixing up to rent out. He led a small group of spiritually hungry believers. I met with them one evening for a Bible study. We looked at 1 Corinthians 13, the chapter in which the Apostle Paul talks about love. It was one of the few New Testament chapters simple enough for me to discuss coherently.

John had my picture taken by a professional photographer and taped an interview with me for a radio show he was hosting. John and his friends seemed to be looking for guidance. They treated me as a traveling apostle.

There were a couple of problems with their perception. I was still very confused about my identity. I was still unclear about my drug-induced delusion of being Jesus. And my moral character was weak. I was attracted to girls my age and lacked self-control.

One day when I was walking around the university campus, I

met a girl who was pretty and smart. We talked about traveling and about God. We went for a drive with some of her friends. Then I brought her back to John's rental house. One kiss led to another, and we crossed the line. I liked her, but I knew what we were doing was wrong.

I felt like a hypocrite. I was acting like a committed Christian around John and his wife, and like an immoral hippie with the girl and her friends. So, a few days later, I said good-bye to the girl, and to John, and continued my trek east.

Confession

I hitchhiked to the next town and walked until I found a church. I was carrying guilt in my heart and wanted to make a confession.

I entered the church office and told the secretary I would like to talk with the pastor. I waited a few minutes and was greeted by a pastor wearing casual slacks and a sports shirt. He invited me into his office. I told him that I needed to make a confession. We sat across from each other as I confessed my sins for the first time to a Protestant pastor.

I told the pastor about my immorality. I knew it was wrong and I wanted the Lord's forgiveness. He listened patiently to me and then we prayed together as I asked the Lord to forgive my sins. I felt better after my confession. I never wanted to have that empty feeling again. I thanked him and walked out.

The next day, I was dropped off at a large turnpike on-ramp in eastern Pennsylvania where the freeways forked in different directions. Some cars were heading toward New York City; others went toward Massachusetts.

Which Way to Go?

A moment of decision had come. I had been vacillating between two options. One was to go to New York City and fly to Europe with a possible trip to Africa. My other option was to go to Massachusetts and then head north into Canada. I could head west through Canada and then go south all the way to Mexico and Central America. Both options seemed interesting, and I couldn't decide which to pursue.

After waiting for over an hour to get a ride, I grew impatient. I made up my mind that I would go where the first car to stop for me was going. If the ride was going toward Massachusetts, I would take it and then head to Canada. If the ride was going toward New York City, I would take it and then head to Europe. When a car finally stopped for me, the driver told me he was heading to New Jersey. It didn't fit my plans exactly, but close enough.

I spent the night in New Jersey with the driver. I was leaning toward flying to Europe, but I was uneasy about it. I decided to phone a psychic whose number I saw in a newspaper. I was vaguely aware that the Bible said psychics were not good, but I wanted assurance that my trip would be safe.

I phoned the psychic's number. An impatient lady told me it would cost five dollars for her to give me advice. I promised I would mail her the money and then told her my concerns. She told me she didn't see any problems in the psychic realm about me going to Europe. I felt foolish after hanging up, but I mailed her the money. The next day, I hitchhiked to the Scandinavian Airlines terminal at JFK airport to buy a standby ticket to Luxembourg.

CHAPTER ELEVEN

ADVENTURES IN EUROPE

In the summer of 1970, standby tickets worked well for both the airlines and thousands of young people heading to Europe. Since many of us were hitchhiking, we could never be sure when we would arrive at the airport. With an eager line of young people willing to wait for the next available seat, the airlines were able to fill up their flights.

I soon found myself flying to the little nation of Luxembourg. I thought about hitchhiking through Europe and living off bread, fruit, and cheese for the next six weeks.

After I landed, I discovered I needed to alter my plan.

I was standing on a freeway on-ramp on the outskirts of the airport in Luxembourg with a half dozen other long-haired travelers. It looked like hitchhiking in America, yet it was different. A steady stream of cars went past us onto the freeway, but nobody stopped.

I asked one of the guys how long he had been waiting for a ride. "I've been here about four hours," he replied. Then motioning his head toward two others, "Those guys have been here since yesterday."

That was all I needed to hear. It was obvious I had to find another way to get around if I was going to have fun traveling through Europe. So much for saving money by hitchhiking. I started walking toward the train station.

Trains, Cars, Bikes

I caught a train from Luxembourg to Brussels. I sat in a second-class car with several other travelers. As we bounced through the countryside, I heard a story that shaped my trip. One American had been traveling around Europe for several months. He told us about a Spanish island called Ibiza in the Mediterranean Sea. "The people on Ibiza are so friendly; they will pull you off the streets and invite you into their homes for dinner. The fruit there is so cheap; half the time the guy at the store tells us just to take it because no coin is small enough to pay for it. The best way to get there is to take a ship from Barcelona."

That sounded great to me. I hadn't planned on it, but Ibiza was now going to be one of my destinations.

A Careless Mistake in Brussels

When I got to Brussels. I walked around, looking for a good place to stay. I met a couple of guys who told me I could stay with them in an abandoned building. They led me to an empty four-story apartment building. We squeezed through a door that was loosely chained to keep people out. The top floor was moldy and gutted. It looked like it was set up for a remodel project that never started. Several people were camped out in the living room of the vacant flat. I put my backpack down in a corner and took off with one of the guys to explore the city.

We walked for several blocks and then split up. I bought some French bread, fruit, and cheese and took it to a bench in a city square for dinner. As night fell, Brussels came alive with interesting characters. This vibrant city had visitors from all over the world. I walked around, looking into cafés and stores. After a few hours I was ready to head back to the abandoned building. I started walking for several blocks before I realized I had a problem. I have a good sense of direction, but the city looked different at night. I thought I had walked back at least as far as I had come that afternoon, but I didn't recognize anything.

I started to get anxious. Everything I had for the trip was in my backpack and I didn't know how to get back to it. I flagged down a cab driver. He didn't speak much English and my French was terrible. I tried to explain to him that I was staying in an abandoned building. That might have narrowed it down to five hundred places for all I knew.

He drove quickly through the streets, stopping occasionally to look back at me. I would look out at the buildings and shake my head "no." He kept driving and I started praying. I felt like a fool for leaving my backpack without writing down the address.

Finally, the cab driver stopped, and I thought the area looked familiar. I got out and paid him and started walking. I turned a corner and found the building. I squeezed through the chained door. The apartment was empty, but my backpack was right where I left it.

The next day, I walked through Brussels carrying my backpack. I found an open-air market with people selling fruit, vegetables, and used goods. I walked past some quality ten-speed bicycles. After negotiations with the seller, I bought one for a few hundred francs, about $100. It would be a strenuous workout to ride a bike with my heavy backpack, but I was on my way to France that afternoon.

Biking in France

Northern France has rolling hills with farms sprinkled along two-lane roads that snake through the countryside. Every few miles the road became cobblestone where clusters of stone houses formed small towns. Each town had its own church, bakery, and shops. Riding a ten-speed bike with thin tires on ancient cobblestones while wearing a backpack was a jarring experience.

I discovered there were youth hostels throughout France. For about five dollars a night, I could always find a room with other guys who were traveling through the countryside.

It took me several days to reach Paris. I remembered it from my previous first-class trip with my grandmother. I was now on a last-class trip, but I was eager to return to one of the world's great cities.

My first night in Paris was disillusioning.

I locked up my bike and walked around the Champs-Élysées. I watched tourists from all over the world. Later that evening, I listened to live chamber music played in a park, and I met a friendly Frenchman who spoke English. The man invited me to come and spend the night at his house. I gladly accepted his invitation, hoping to save money and get to know a new friend at the same time. We took the subway across town to the stop near his house. When we emerged onto the street, he asked me to wait a few minutes at the subway exit while he went to make sure everything was okay at his house. I thought that was a little strange, but I waited patiently. I kept waiting for more than an hour. I finally realized he wasn't coming back. In hindsight, he must have had a wife or mother who didn't want a stranger in the house. By then, it was after midnight. I was tired and angry at the man who had just burned me. I started walking down the street, not sure where I was going. The street led me to a spot overlooking the Seine River.

I walked down toward the water, where I saw boxes and cargo crates along the riverbank. I heard someone snoring as I walked past a large crate. I assumed this was a place homeless guys spent the night. I kept walking and found an empty crate set apart from the others. I could now tell people that I once had a place on the Left Bank of the Seine River.

Exploring Paris

The next morning, I retrieved my bike and found a youth hostel where I could stay for a few days. I wandered from the hostel each morning until I found an outdoor café serving coffee and breakfast. I would order *café au lait* [coffee with milk]. French coffee was so potent I could feel it waking me up on the spot. It was served with a free basket of fresh croissants with butter and jam. I would eat the entire basket of croissants for the price of a cup of coffee. An abundance of hungry American hippies was probably one reason most cafés stopped giving out free croissants a few years later.

Getting around in Paris was a challenge. I had taken two years of French in high school, but the cheating I did back then caught up with me. At times, in Paris subway stations, I would ask at least three people for directions. I needed to get two or three people sending me in the same direction before I was confident they weren't sending me on a wild goose chase.

I enjoyed the Louvre on the trip with my grandmother when I was thirteen years old, so I went to visit the magnificent museum again. I went first to see the Mona Lisa. She looked about the same as she did seven years earlier; however, next to her and not getting near the attention was another painting by Leonardo de Vinci that captivated me. John the Baptist was pointing his finger skyward, indicating that Christ was the One who warranted our complete attention and devotion. For the first time in my life, I felt like God was speaking to me through a piece of art.

I returned to the Louvre the next day and spent more time staring at the picture of John the Baptist. Its message that Christ is the one sent by God spoke deeply to my heart.

After another couple of days touring the city and several more baskets of croissants, I got on my bike to continue south toward Spain.

A Friendly French Girl

In a country town south of Paris, I met a friendly French girl. She couldn't speak much English, and my French was *un petit peu* [a little bit]. We tried to talk, but we had to use sign language, so we just walked around her town for the evening until I headed off to sleep in a nearby field.

I didn't get far down the road on my bike the next morning when a car zoomed past me, honking. The car pulled over to the side of the road. The girl I had met the night before got out of the car and started walking toward me. She was traveling with her sister and brother-in-law. They were heading to the south of France and offered me a ride.

We took the bike wheels off, put the bike in the trunk, and took off. We were on two-lane country roads with cars, trucks, bicyclists, and occasional pedestrians.

I thought this was going to be fun, but the brother-in-law nearly killed us. He drove fast and furiously. He careened around any slow traffic we came across. Sometimes he passed them on the left, and other times, if someone was coming toward us, he passed on the right using the dirt shoulder of the road. At times, I was certain we were going to die. A few times, cars going north passed cars at the same time we were passing a car going south. The passing cars were off the road, almost in the ditches, driving at over sixty miles an hour.

We camped that night on a grassy field somewhere in the country. After a dinner around the campfire, we rolled out our sleeping bags. It soon became apparent the French girl was planning to sleep with me. I knew it was wrong, but I cooperated with her. It was an experience I have never forgotten—and not because of the romance. I have never forgotten how empty it made me feel. We had no real love for each other and almost no communication. As inexcusable as my conduct was, the emptiness of it was something I never wanted to forget, because I never wanted to experience it again.

The next day, they dropped me off in Southern France and I started riding toward Nice, on the French Riviera. I found a youth hostel where I met an American girl with a car. She was touring the countryside. She was a natural beauty, with mid-length blond hair. I was really attracted to her as we drove through the wheat fields and rolling hills of southern France.

After a couple of hours, we came upon a large cathedral. We parked and began to walk through the vast sanctuary. We had been talking when we entered the sanctuary, but within a few minutes I was distracted. I felt the spiritual reality that I was in a place where thousands of people had prayed over several hundred years. I could feel the presence of the Holy Spirit, though at the time, it simply felt like a very holy place, like God was in the building.

After a few minutes I glanced over at the girl who had driven me there. Her beauty seemed to fade in comparison to the awesome presence of the Lord in the cathedral. She seemed to recognize that I had another priority that she did not share. We parted ways later that day.

I knew then that my deepest desire was to get close to the Lord.

Headed for Spain by Motorbike

In Nice, I met a man at a hostel who sold me his motorbike. I paid him half the money he wanted and assured him I would mail him a check for the other half when I got back to the United States. I then sold my bicycle to a man at the hostel for the same price I paid for it and headed from Nice toward Spain on the motorbike. I had thought this would be a great way to travel, but it was awkward riding a motorbike while wearing a backpack with a sleeping bag attached. The wind resistance on my pack made it feel like I was being dragged down from behind by the weight on my back.

I sold the motorbike in Marseilles and continued to Spain by train. The brown hills and oak trees of the Spanish countryside reminded me of Marin County. After six weeks on the road, I was starting to miss home.

Exploring Spain

The picturesque Mediterranean houses along the Costa Brava north of Barcelona lured me to get off the train and start exploring. I spent several days swimming in the Mediterranean and sleeping on the beach at night.

I visited several old churches in Spain with stained glass windows, ornate altars, and crucifixes. I have been fascinated by the crucifix ever since my mother gave me an ivory and teak one when I was young. As a boy, I often held it when I prayed beside my bed. When I looked at the figure of Jesus on the cross, I was impressed with how much He loved me. I never felt worthy of the sacrifice He made for me. I would often walk into an empty Catholic sanctuary and kneel at a pew, gaze at the crucifix, and confess my sins.

One Catholic sanctuary on the Costa Brava was unique. In the place above the altar, where every Catholic church has a crucifix, this sanctuary had a statue of Jesus with his arms extended wide. He was not on the cross at all. It was a symbol of His resurrection. I stood in stunned silence as I considered the implications that statue represented. Jesus did not remain on the cross suffering for our sins. After the cross, He rose from the dead. He was alive!

Early one morning, as I slept on the sand in my sleeping bag,

I was awakened by a sharp kick. I looked up and saw two soldiers, members of the Guardia Civil, carrying carbines. One of them spoke to me in Spanish. I couldn't understand his words, but I had an instant "interpretation of tongues." He was telling me that hippies were not welcome to camp on this beach. I quickly rolled up my sleeping bag and walked into town.

By then, I was almost out of money, so I took a train to Barcelona to find a telephone company to call my mother to wire money. There was a Western Union office in downtown Barcelona. It took a train, a bus, and a lot of walking to find it. I thought wiring money would be a quick, simple process. However, in 1970, wiring money internationally took a lot longer than I had expected.

It was Friday. The large bottom floor of the telephone office was filled with dozens of phone booths and hundreds of travelers waiting in line to place long distance calls all over the world. I waited for more than an hour, listening to people shout in languages I couldn't understand.

When my turn finally came, I made a collect call to my mother. It was a joy to hear her voice. She was raising my younger brothers and sisters alone, and working full time as a social worker, yet she always had time to help me when I needed her. She told me she would go to the bank on Monday and have them wire me the money.

After a couple of hours in the phone office, I walked and took a bus back to the train station. I then discovered that the last train up the coast had already departed. I would have to wait until morning to catch another train.

I was unsure where to spend the night until I saw a couple of travelers asleep on benches just outside the train station. I followed their examples. They had their backpacks tied to their arms, so a thief would have to wake them up to steal their backpacks. It was hard to sleep on the bench, but I was almost out of money and it was free.

The next morning, I headed north on a train to a small town on the Costa Brava. I looked in vain for a good deal at a youth hostel, and then took my chances that the Guardia Civil would not be checking every beach up and down the coast.

During the next few days, I swam in the warm blue Mediterranean Sea and ate fresh bread, cheese, and fruit from the local shops. I discovered a sweet, cold, healthy drink called *Horchata de Chufa*. At night, I rolled my sleeping bag out in the sand on the beach and slept under the stars. Soon, I headed back to Barcelona to get the money my mother had promised to wire to me.

I arrived at the Western Union office late in the afternoon only to find that the money had not arrived. I didn't want to spend another night in the train station. With my money running out, the beach was the best place to sleep. I knew I had to hurry if I was going to catch the last train back to the Costa Brava.

I started jogging through the streets of Barcelona, weaving erratically through the people strolling along the sidewalks. As I jogged as fast as possible, a Bible verse started going through my mind:

> Behold, I lay in Zion a stone, a precious cornerstone.
> Those who believeth in Him will not make haste
> (Isaiah 28:16 [KJV]).

Like a song that keeps running through your mind, this verse kept coming back to me. As soon as I thought of it, I started an argument in my head. *I know I should trust in you Lord, but I'm going to miss the train if I don't hurry, and it will be miserable sleeping on a bench again. I have to make haste this time!* People stopped and stared at me as I careened past them. My backpack was weighing me down, but this time, I was desperate to catch the last train out of Barcelona.

I got exhausted, so I stopped and waved at a cab passing by. The driver pulled over and I told him I needed to go to the train station as fast as possible. As he inched along in traffic, the scripture came back to me. *Those who believeth in Him shall not make haste.* I shook off the scripture and leaned forward to speak to the driver in Spanglish. "Pronto, pronto! I'm late to get the train."

He finally got my message and began driving aggressively around cars and speeding through the city. We arrived at the train station at 4:50, which I thought was just in the nick of time. Then, I saw the long line of people waiting to purchase tickets.

I was in survival mode at that point. I walked down the length of the line toward the ticket booth. Near the front of the line, I cut in ahead of someone who wasn't paying attention. It was a classic ugly-American move, but I thought it was necessary to catch the train. I got my ticket just before five o'clock and started running down the platform. The engines were already revving, and the train was full of people when I jumped aboard. There were no seats left open, so I plopped my backpack down next to another couple of men who were sitting on the floor between two train cars.

I was so relieved to be on board that a seat on the floor did not bother me at all. As I began to relax, more people stepped onto the train. We were full, yet every minute or two, someone else would squeeze on board. It was getting hot on the crammed floor. Finally, the train began to move. I wanted to cheer. It went forward about ten yards and stopped. I could see one of the conductors walking down the platform. He helped a few more people get onto the train steps. For some reason we weren't going anywhere. It was so crowded on the floor that my knees were up against my chest. For another forty-five minutes we just sat and waited, like hot, crowded cattle going to slaughter.

Then the scripture came back to me once again, *Those who believe in Him will not make haste.* I realized I could have walked to the train station, waited patiently in line, and still had a place on this train floor. I asked the Lord to forgive me for not trusting him and listening to the Word. Soon after that little prayer, the whistle blew, the train shuddered, and slowly chugged down the track toward the Costa Brava.

On my third trip to the Western Union office in Barcelona, the money my mother sent had arrived. After two weeks on the Costa Brava beaches, I was ready to move on. I splurged that night on a little hotel room and washed some of my clothes in the sink.

No Joy in Ibiza

The next day, I went to buy a ticket to Ibiza, the island I had heard about on the train from Luxembourg to Brussels. I had to wait two more days before there was room on a ship for me to buy a third-class ticket. That should have been a warning to me. I slept on the deck on board a large ship as we crossed the

Mediterranean Sea. I peered down on the nicely dressed people on the first-class deck below, wondering how it would feel to cruise in luxury.

Ibiza is a Mediterranean island with Spanish architecture. The white houses with red tile roofs and cobblestone streets make it look like a postcard city. Evidently, the guy I met on the train had told a lot of people about the secret of Ibiza, because the island was packed with travelers.

Worse, nobody offered me free fruit or a nice place to stay. Food was expensive, and there was no room at the local hostel. After wandering around the main city, I took a small boat taxi to a campground on the far side of the island. The campground was full as well; so, after taking a swim in the warm water, I joined a couple of guys in search of somewhere to sleep. We eventually found a place to spend the night on a rocky outcropping overlooking the back side of the island.

It was too hot and humid to get into my sleeping bag, so I tried to sleep on top of it. Mosquitoes attacked me throughout the night. Every time I rolled over to try to slap a mosquito, I would be jabbed in the back with one of the sharp rocks beneath me.

It was time to go home.

CHAPTER TWELVE

GOING HOME AGAIN

I took trains from Spain back to Luxembourg and flew back to New York City.

I was determined to go back to Marin and get my life settled on a firm foundation. I couldn't help others until I understood what my life was supposed to be about. I planned to start going to Bible studies on a regular basis and find a church where I could learn and grow. I also hoped to finish my classes and graduate from College of Marin.

Driving to Dallas

On the plane flight back to New York, I sat by a lady and her young son. As we talked, she told me her car was in New York and she planned to drive straight through to Dallas when we landed. She invited me to join her and share the driving. I immediately accepted her offer. I assumed it would be cheaper for me to fly to San Francisco from Dallas than from New York. It was not one of my best money-saving decisions.

We had talked so much on the eight-hour flight to JFK, that I only slept an hour or so on the plane. We went through customs in New York and took a taxi to her parked car. She wanted to drive the first leg of our trip and then let me take over. We were both excited to be back in the United States. It is a blessing to speak English and feel secure in our legal system.

We talked nonstop as we drove from New York into Pennsylvania. As darkness fell, she told me she was exhausted. It was my turn to drive while she slept. She pulled over and climbed into the back seat, next to her sleeping son.

The plan was for me to drive through the night while she slept. Then I could sleep the next day while she drove. I got in the driver's seat and headed back onto the highway. Within minutes she was fast asleep, and my adrenaline ran out. I was so tired I thought I was going to fall asleep at the wheel. I wanted to keep driving because she was counting on me, but I knew it was too dangerous. I pulled off the freeway and found an office park nearby with a nice lawn. I unrolled my sleeping bag on the lawn and fell fast asleep.

The sun was well up the next morning when I woke up. The lady was standing over me looking refreshed and happy. I explained to her that I needed to get a little more sleep, as we got back into the car. She took the wheel as we headed back onto the freeway.

"Where are we, in Kentucky?" she asked, with a smile.

"No. I don't think so." I replied.

"In Tennessee?" she asked again.

"I don't think so."

"Then where are we? How far did you drive?"

Just about then, we passed a sign saying we were still in Pennsylvania. I tried to explain how tired I had been and how I didn't want to endanger us by falling asleep. She was really upset. She scolded me and then went quiet for many hours. As far as she was concerned, she had picked up a flake on the plane and she regretted it.

I did end up helping with some driving, but I was still jet-lagged from Europe. We made it to her house in Dallas after a few days. She took me to the airport the next morning. I was glad to be heading home, but there were no standby tickets available to San Francisco. I had to pay full fare and didn't save any money at all.

Still Searching for Truth

I returned to live with my mom and brothers and sisters. I now was more serious than ever in my search for truth and God.

I went back to Bible studies on Tuesdays at the house on Greenfield in San Rafael. I also attended a metaphysical church, a Christian Science church, and Bahá'í meetings. I wanted to find God and learn from anyone who knew him. I didn't have any friends in these groups, but friendship was secondary to truth for me.

I signed up for twenty-three units at College of Marin when the semester started shortly after my return. On one of the first days of classes, I was hitchhiking from Terra Linda to Kentfield when I got a ride from a hefty man in a low-riding Chevy. He had black wraparound sunglasses and long sideburns. He had recently moved to Marin from Chicago. After a few miles, I started talking to him about Jesus.

He looked sideways at me as he drove and listened to my witness about Christ. Then, just as if he hadn't heard a word I had said, he started telling me about Jesus. He told me he was Jewish and was a missionary. He invited me to visit him and the new group he had just started.

We exchanged names when he dropped me off. His name

was Marty Rosen. A few years later he changed it to the Hebrew name Moishe. The group he founded only had six people when I met him. It was called Jews for Jesus. Moishe and I started a friendship that day that lasted for forty years, until he went to be with the Lord in 2010. Jews for Jesus grew into an international missions agency that has been more effective in bringing Jews to Christ than any other organization.

CHAPTER THIRTEEN

GOD'S PROVISION

Some things in life must be sought after. They must be diligently pursued in order to be attained. Other things come to you before you even know how much you are going to need them. Some of the most important things that have come my way over the years seemed to have been dropped into my life from above.

A Chevy Van

Soon after I returned home from Europe, my Rhode Island friend, Bruce, showed up at our house with a Chevy van. Bruce and one of his friends were on their way to Hawaii. They told me they needed money in order to buy their airline tickets. Bruce offered to sell me his Chevy van. The van was blue, almost new, and in great shape. It was paneled and carpeted on the inside. I told him all I had was $1,100 after my trip to Europe. He was hoping to get more for it, but he accepted what I had and left for Hawaii the next day.

It was a relief for me to be out of money for the first time since I was a child. My money supply had felt tainted ever since I had started cheating my paper route customers and poker friends. Now that it was all gone, I felt I could start over with a clear conscience. I was ready to reapply for my driver's license and get a job.

Trident Builders

I got more than a job. I became the owner of a small company called Trident Builders.

My parents were now divorced, and my dad was living with his girlfriend, Loel. Loel was working for a lady who owned an answering service. This lady had a daughter, who had a boyfriend, who was a carpenter. The lady ran a *Yellow Pages* ad for her daughter's boyfriend and called his company Trident Builders. The ad said: *Trident Builders makes quality fences, decks, and retaining walls. No job too small.* The ad generated five to seven calls every week from Marin County residents looking to have work done. They lived in some of the most expensive homes in America.

After the owner's daughter broke up with the boy and he left the county, Loel called me and asked if I was interested in owning a little company called Trident Builders. I needed a job and did not lack confidence, so I accepted the offer.

There were, however, a few problems to overcome. I had never built a fence, deck, or retaining wall in my life. Nor did I own any tools. I went to my parents' cabinet and looked at the tools my dad had left when he moved out. I found two old hammers, a level, and a handsaw.

My dad was not good with tools. His gift was making friends who were good at fixing cars, dishwashers, or fences. He would invite them over for dinner and a couple of beers. They, in turn, helped him fix what was broken around our house.

So, following in his footsteps, I walked down the street and made an offer to my friend Phil Zito to join me in Trident Builders. Phil's dad had a few tools as well, and I knew Phil was better at building things than I was, because he had helped his dad work on projects around their house. I had spent several Saturday mornings working at Phil's house to help with his chores when we were young, so he could be free to go out and play.

Phil accepted my offer to join Trident Builders.

Our First Job

The first job Phil and I went out to estimate was for a man who asked us if we had pictures of fences we had built. Obviously, we didn't, but that didn't stop us. We went to the local hardware store and bought a *Better Homes and Gardens Fences* book. We showed the man the fancy fences in the book.

Fortunately, he didn't pick one. He told us that he actually wanted a fence like the one his neighbor had built across the street. That was perfect for us. We walked across the street and measured the boards of his neighbor's fence. (I didn't know the difference between a 2x4 and a 4x4 until we did those measurements.) We then went to a local lumberyard to ask more details about how a fence was built.

We got the job and built our first fence, which took us about a week. We were riding high when we cashed our first check.

Trident Builders got almost every job we estimated, because we had the lowest overhead possible. Phil and I both lived in our parents' homes and ate their food. We estimated our labor at four dollars per hour, with no benefits, taxes, recordkeeping, or insurance.

We added 10 percent of the gross to our estimates, which we paid to the lady who placed our ad in the *Yellow Pages.*

We soon learned that some jobs were more challenging than others. We also discovered it can be costly to get jobs when you don't know how to do them. One of our early jobs was building a flight of cement stairs to a backyard patio at a hillside home in Ignacio. The slope was about twenty steps up a steep incline in the backyard. The steps were supposed to be done with an exposed aggregate surface.

Every afternoon, when our classes at College of Marin were over, Phil and I drove up to Ignacio and worked on framing for the steps. It should have been a two-day job, but after two weeks we were stumped. So, we called in reinforcements. Phil's older brother, Mike, spent several hours showing us how to make the forms to hold the concrete for the stairs. It took us most of another week to finally get ready for the concrete.

Then we lost a couple of days' work to a rainstorm, which caused unintended consequences.

We had the landscape supply company dump 6,000 pounds of sand and gravel on the driveway. We rented a cement mixer and spent a day mixing cement and pouring it into buckets to carry around to the backyard. As we attempted to walk up the rain-soaked hill, carrying fifty-pound buckets of wet cement, we began to slip down the slope and spilled several buckets of cement.

Mixing one shovelful of cement for every four shovels of sand and gravel on the driveway of a nice hillside home for the first time in your life is not a pretty sight. By the end of the second day of cement work, the house and yard looked like a giant had dropped a cement bomb on the property.

The homeowner became concerned. At the end of the week, he called for a meeting with Phil and me. He began by telling us the aggregate we had put into the cement was already chipping out. That was bad news. He then told us that he wanted to talk with the president of Trident Builders. I didn't have the heart to tell him that I was the president of Trident Builders. I was also the CFO, the chairman of the board, and the janitor; Phil was the vice president. What we did tell him was that we would fix the aggregate problem and clean everything up before we were done. We didn't tell him that we had no idea how we were going to do this.

So, Phil and I headed back to the materials company that sold the gravel and cement. We asked for their counsel. They sold us big steel chisels to chip out all the aggregate from every step. They also told us to bury the aggregate under a layer of cement and then lightly brush away the top layer of cement after it had dried for a couple of hours.

It took three days to chip away a deep enough layer in the dried cement stairs to get enough depth to replace the aggregate properly. Finally, a few weeks later, we completed what should have been a three-day job. After hiring Mike, paying for steel chisels, additional cement and aggregate, as well as a month's worth of gas, I figured we made about twenty-five cents an hour for that backbreaking mess of a job.

This would not be the worse job I got us into before I finally retired from our construction business. Nevertheless, despite several learning experiences like this, we prospered. Trident Builders became my main source of income for several years.

CHAPTER FOURTEEN

SPIRITUAL
TURNING POINT

One afternoon after classes, I hiked up the water-tank hill in Terra Linda near my mother's house. I thought I would take some time to pray. It took twenty minutes to get up the winding trail through the trees to the top of the hill. After admiring the view, I sat down on some wild grasses and began to pray. Five minutes later, I was through praying and sat thinking about what I would do next.

It didn't seem like my prayer time had accomplished much. I was in no hurry to head back down the hill, because I didn't have any friends I wanted to see that afternoon. I didn't fit in with the Christians, and most of my old friends were still doing dope. I started thinking about a verse in 1 Peter 3: *The eyes of the Lord are on the righteous and His ear is open to their cry.*

I reasoned that God was going to see me and hear me because Jesus had cleansed me from my sin and made me righteous in God's sight. If this was a fact, then my prayer time should be very significant. I decided to try to pray again. Only this time I was going to act like I was actually in God's presence and He was listening to everything I was saying.

I turned toward the hillside as I knelt down. I imagined myself going before the Lord like a man would approach the throne of a king. I prayed with intensity as if God would grant me everything I asked for. I prayed for the war in Vietnam, my family, and our little Bible study ministry. After a while, I opened my eyes. I felt as if I was in a worship service and the presence of the Holy Spirit was surrounding me. I realized that the Lord had heard my prayer. This was a turning point for me spiritually.

I became excited to return to the top of the water-tank hill the next day for another session of prayer. I didn't experience the same intensity of the Spirit's presence, but it didn't matter. From then on, I felt like I had a friend I could go visit any time I wanted. God had shown me prayer was the key to my relationship with Him. Sometimes, He would fill me with grace and peace on the mountain. Other times, I was simply content to know I had poured out my heart to the One who can change the world.

From then until now, my prayer time alone with the Lord has been the most important part of my life. In those times, the Lord has given me revelation, grace, and strength to minister to others and deal with every trial in my life.

Deliverance from Demons

My life seemed to be going well. I was enjoying our construction work. I was studying the Word and evangelizing. I was no longer getting stoned. And I was growing more confident in my relationship with the Lord. However, I was surprised by what came next.

One evening, Randy McAtee took me to meet Peter and

Bronik, two brothers who had started a ministry in San Anselmo. When we arrived, they were with friends, listening intently to a cassette tape recording of a missionary. They invited us to sit down to listen with them. I soon realized the missionary was casting demons out of people. Even though I knew it had happened in the Bible, I had never heard of demons being cast out of people in modern times.

Within a few minutes, I began to feel nauseous. I heard the preacher commanding demons to leave people. His loud, authoritative voice made me feel sick inside. Just before I stood up to leave, Bronik stopped the tape player. He looked at me and asked how I was doing. I told him that I felt sick to my stomach. He explained that this was a sign that I might need deliverance from spirits. Everyone was looking at me as I assured them I was already feeling better and would probably be fine.

Bronik restarted the tape. I heard the preacher command another demon to leave someone. I felt like I was about to throw up, so I told them, "I'm getting sick."

Bronik stopped the tape and asked if they could pray for me. I nodded a *yes*.

Before they prayed, he asked me if I had been involved in any occult activity. I told them about my experiences with séances, channeling spirits, and my great-grandmother's signet ring.

Peter and Bronik then commanded every demonic spirit that had come into me to leave me in Jesus' name. As soon as they gave that command, I fell from my chair to the floor into a fetal position. I became sick to my stomach at the same time. For the next fifteen minutes I had one of the most powerful spiritual experiences of my life. I realized the reality of demonic spirits and their evil power for the first time. What I thought had been sins with little consequence, I now saw in an entirely new light. I understood that my occult activity, my drug taking, and my immorality had all given demons access to my soul.

As the demonic forces left me, I began to feel great relief. I had clarity about the reality of good and evil that I had never known before. The embarrassment I felt about being on the floor and throwing up in front of the group gave way to thankfulness. I was thankful they loved the Lord and loved me enough to pray me through one of the most important steps in my walk with Christ.

I left Bronik's apartment with a new sense of the fear of the Lord and a desire to bring the good news of Jesus to as many people as possible. I knew many of my peers were entering the dark world controlled by demons every day. I wanted God to use me to bring them freedom in Christ. Those opportunities came soon, though they didn't always work out smoothly.

A Dangerous Encounter

In the early 1970s, San Francisco was drawing gurus and cult leaders, along with wannabe hippies and drug dealers from around the world. As the years went by, the streets of the Haight-Ashbury district and the lawns of Golden Gate Park were filled with thousands of people whose lives were damaged by their experimentation with sex, drugs, and false religion.

Randy and I went into San Francisco one afternoon to hand out tracts and share our faith at a large anti-war rally in Golden Gate Park. Thousands of people gathered on a huge lawn in the park. Many spread blankets on the grass, smoking weed and picnicking, while listening to rock bands and speakers. Randy and I walked through the crowd, handing people tracts about Jesus. We stopped to talk with anyone who was open to talking with us. We were bold in our approach, and started many conversations by asking, "Do you know Jesus is alive?"

One guy responded by asking me, "Is that a new song by The Doobie Brothers?"

As we walked through the Golden Gate Park crowd that afternoon, I noticed a tanned and bearded man wearing a loincloth and turban. He was sitting in a full lotus yoga position with his eyes closed. I stopped to ask him if he knew that Jesus was alive, but he didn't respond. I stared at him and wondered if he was in a demonic trance. Randy and I split up as we moved on to talk with people closer to the stage. We ran out of tracts after a while because so many people took them from us.

As I moved back away from the stage area, I was looking for Randy, who had wandered away in the crowd. I walked past the turbaned man who was still sitting in the lotus position with his legs crossed, his hands facing upwards on his knees, and his eyes closed. I could hear him chanting "OM." I stopped and decided to make a better attempt at sharing Christ with him. "Excuse me. Do you know that Jesus is alive?"

He continued chanting "OM" and didn't respond. I wasn't sure he could hear me because the music from the stage was loud. I crouched down so my face was a few inches from his and spoke louder. "Excuse me. Do you know that Jesus is alive?"

His "OM" grew louder.

"Excuse me . . . ," I persisted.

"OM. . . ."

At this point, I was convinced that he was demon-possessed and needed deliverance. I stood up and started to walk away. A moment later, I did something I would never recommend anyone doing to an uncooperative person. I turned back around, crouched down to his level, and commanded the demon to leave him.

"Demon, I command you to leave this man in Jesus' name!"

He had been saying "OM" loudly, but when I again commanded the demon to leave, he shrieked, grabbed me around the neck, and screamed, "OM!"

He had me in a bear hug with his arms around my neck. He squeezed me tightly as he kept screaming. People in the crowd started to form a circle around us. I didn't know what to do. I had a strong impulse to punch him in the side as hard as I could, but I was supposed to be telling people about Jesus. It wasn't going to look good for a Christian to be in a fight. It could be a fight to the death between me and the demon-possessed yogi once I started punching.

Just then, I heard Randy's voice. "I command you to release him in Jesus' name!"

Randy shouted again with authority. "I command you to release him right now!"

Suddenly, the guy let me go. I stood up as fast as I could. Randy and I then walked through the throng of people surrounding us. The band was still playing on the stage, people all around us were still getting stoned, and I was glad to be walking away with only a sore neck. We had planted a lot of seeds in people's hearts, had some great conversations, and learned a good lesson about leaving chanting demoniacs alone.

As we walked back to our car, someone handed Randy a flyer for a nearby meeting with Jim Jones. Jim was the false-teaching cult leader who would commit suicide with more than 900 of his followers a few years later. One of my friends who attended a Jim Jones service told me about the experience. Not only would Jones stage fake healings to fool his unsuspecting followers, but in their meetings, they sang the same songs we used to worship Jesus, like "He Is Lord." However, the focus of their songs was Jones, not Jesus.

PART IV

LIVING FOR JESUS

CHAPTER FIFTEEN

JOINING THE JESUS MOVEMENT

Kent Philpott was one of the key leaders who sparked a new spiritual movement in the San Francisco Bay Area in the late 1960s. Kent was a seminary student at Golden Gate Baptist in Marin County in 1967 when he began evangelizing in the Haight-Ashbury district of San Francisco. By 1968, other seminary students joined Kent serving Jesus on the streets of San Francisco. Thousands of young people had flocked to San Francisco that year—the flower children who came seeking "peace, love, and happiness." They tried to find enlightenment with the aid of marijuana, LSD, and new age religion.

By 1970, this movement had gained momentum. Even though Kent and his wife, Bobbie, had three young children, they opened their home on Greenfield Avenue in San Rafael to three girls who were young disciples. Paul Bryant, another student at Golden Gate Seminary, opened a rented house for men in San Anselmo. Their houses and several others became gathering places for weekly Bible studies, as well as places to live for young people who wanted to grow closer to Jesus.

Attending Weekly Bible Study

By 1970, Kent had moved his weekly Bible study to a United Methodist church in San Anselmo. When I returned from Europe, I started attending these Tuesday night meetings, but I didn't feel like I fit in. Most people in the meeting could quote the Bible and find passages to share, while I didn't know one end of the Bible from the other. However, I kept showing up every Tuesday night because I wanted to get to know Jesus the way they knew him.

At these meetings, Kent led worship on his guitar. He taught the Scriptures in a way that helped me understand them for the first time in my life. I have a bad singing voice, but I sang along in the meetings. It was wonderful to experience worship for the first time in my life and to have Bible teachings that strengthened my faith.

Kent continued weekly street evangelizing along with many of these young disciples. Every week, new people were crowded onto sofas or sat on the floor in large living rooms in the discipleship houses to worship and hear the Word. Most of them had long hair and wore headbands. Many had come from around the country seeking enlightenment from the hippies. Some believers moved in together and formed discipleship houses.

For most of them, like me, learning about Jesus was a new experience. Some of us had heard parts of the gospel in the Catholic Church but never understood the gospel of God's grace. The total church attendance in Marin County in the early '70s was less than five percent of the population.

As I look back, preaching the gospel in Marin County in the 1970s was like fishing for trout in a mountain stream where no one had fished for years. If no one has fished for them before, undisturbed trout bite on worms, lures, flies, or almost anything you put on a hook.

At almost every Bible study or church service where there was contemporary worship and the gospel was preached in the Bay Area, young people accepted Christ. Many of them became "on fire" and began to share their faith. Because they were sharing their testimonies about being delivered from drugs and the occult, more young people came to know Jesus. From 1969 to 1972, this same spiritual awakening was happening in cities across the nation. Recognizing this, *TIME* magazine sent a reporter to interview several of us for a major story. Their June 21, 1971, cover story called our revival "The Jesus Movement."

Solid Rock Discipleship House

In early November, Bob Gaulden was the speaker at the Tuesday night Bible study. At the end of the meeting Kent called me over to talk with Bob and him. Bob, who was about my age, was a strong disciple. He was planning to get married and open a new discipleship house in Novato after the first of the year. Kent thought the Lord wanted me to move in with Bob when the house opened. This was an unexpected challenge.

For a couple of weeks, I struggled with the decision of whether to move into the new discipleship house. I was sharing a bedroom with my three younger brothers and paying my mom $100 a month for rent. I was also continuing to attend the College of Marin and doing construction work for Trident Builders. I was in a pretty good routine and didn't want to break it. I was also helping my mother by cooking dinners for our family, since she didn't get home from work until six o'clock every evening.

Then, during one of my daily Bible reading times, I came across verses that changed my life.

> "Truly I tell you," Jesus replied, "no one who has left home or brothers or sisters or mother or father or children or fields for me and the gospel will fail to receive a hundred times as much in this present age: homes, brothers, sisters, mothers, children and fields—along with persecutions—and in the age to come eternal life. But many who are first will be last, and the last first" (Mark 10:29–31).

I read these verses over and over. Jesus was making a promise that I would receive a hundred times as much if I left my home, brothers, sisters, and mother for Him.

At that time in my life, the only way I knew how to determine if the scriptures were true continued to be to test them. If Jesus said "Forgive," then I tried forgiving. If the Bible said, "Give," then I tried giving. If Jesus said, "Be my witness," I told others about Christ. So I decided to test the Lord and see what would happen if I left my family and moved into the discipleship house to grow closer to the Lord.

I loaded my clothes into a big box and drove my truck to 508 Wilson Avenue in Novato on February 6, 1971, the day Solid Rock opened with Bob Gaulden as the leader. I moved in with Bob, two other men, and two women.

Holding Our Possessions in Common

The first night, we held a meeting and decided to "hold all things in common," just like the disciples in Acts 2:44–47. This meant we would share our cars, our clothes, and any money we made while we were living together. Holding our possessions in common was a radical step for us to take and it had a profound effect on me. I had been a greedy kid and saved my money to spend on myself. It was a big step for me to work hard all week and then turn the money over to our house leaders to be shared with everyone.

When we held meetings at Solid Rock, I began trying to share my faith in Christ. However, I was not as comfortable talking about the Bible as other believers because I knew so little about it.

Early on, after one meeting, two older couples were talking in our dining room. I walked up and listened as one of the ladies told the others about a problem she was going through. As they listened quietly, I thought I had the solution to her problem. I chimed in by quoting one of the few scriptures I knew. "Romans 8:28 says, *'All things work together for the good for those who love God and are called according to His purpose.'*"

I was expecting them to thank me for the great insight. Instead, the lady who was speaking looked at me with disgust and responded, "I hate it when Christians use that verse to give such superficial answers to problems." The others did not speak up. They seemed to agree with her.

I walked away feeling confused that my first attempt to use a scripture verse to help a believer had been rebuked rather than praised. I had a lot to learn about having compassion for hurting people; nevertheless, Romans 8:28 has helped me many times over the years.

Living at Solid Rock had many benefits and challenges. I had never been around people who read their Bibles and prayed regularly, so it was a big help for me to listen to people quote scripture as part of their regular conversations. As the months went on, I became more familiar with many scriptures—where to find them and what they really meant. It was also a big help to be around people who were not drinking or using marijuana.

Everyone needs friends, and having friends who were saved and sober helped me resist the temptation to go back to drugs and immorality.

However, a number of things got complicated due to the sharing of our money and possessions. It can be blessing, but it can also be dangerous if you don't have good communication.

I had brought my blue panel truck to Solid Rock. Others had brought their cars and trucks as well. Sometimes I would go out to our driveway and find that someone had taken my truck into town to do an errand. I would then use whatever car was available.

One afternoon, Malcolm Dawes, one of the other residents, and I got into one of the cars parked in our driveway and headed down Indian Valley Road. I was driving fast as we entered a turn on the twisting road. Suddenly, the car fell sharply off the right side of the road. I hit the brakes and we skidded to a stop.

The car was sloping down toward the shoulder of the road as we sat in stunned silence. We climbed out of the car to see what had happened. As we walked to the right side of the car, we saw that both tires on that side were gone! They had fallen off the car and careened through the bushes as we had made the turn.

After we walked back to Solid Rock, we learned that one of the guys had been rotating the tires on the car. He got distracted and left the car before putting the lug nuts back on the passenger side wheels. We had been driving a car with two wheels ready to fall off.

The practice of sharing our lives and possessions wasn't perceived by all our house members in the same way.

We had house-painting and construction crews at Solid Rock. I led the construction crew, and two of the men worked with me at Trident Builders. Some weeks I was working as many as sixty hours.

One day before we left for work, I asked Laura, who lived in the house with us, if she would do my laundry while I was working. I thought she had some time to help me since she stayed home to prepare meals and clean while the men were doing construction or painting. Laura looked me in the eye and declared, "No. You do your own laundry. I'm not doing it."

I was upset. My business brought in most of the money to pay for our rent, the food, and everything we needed to live on. I couldn't believe Laura was going to give me a bad time about doing my laundry. However, she remained steadfast. I did my own laundry and wrestled with resentment. As I prayed about forgiving Laura, the Lord gave me a message that has helped me to this day:

"Only do what you have the grace to do without feeling like you are entitled to special consideration, or else you will become bitter and resentful."

In later years, when I was upset that others on our church staff did not seem to be working as hard as I was, the wisdom from that message would return to me. I should only do or give what I could give freely in my service to the Lord, because there was no guarantee that others around me would be giving in the same way. This approach has helped me stay free from resentment over the years.

Healing Tears

Shortly after I moved into Solid Rock, I attended Bob and Carol Gaulden's wedding in San Jose. It was the first time I had witnessed the marriage ceremony of two people who were both dedicated to Christ. Their marriage stirred me deeply. I hadn't cried for a couple of years, but the power of a holy God was present in their ceremony. My tears began to flow as Carol's dad walked her down the aisle of the church.

One Saturday morning soon thereafter, I walked up the street from Solid Rock to find a quiet place to pray. I went north on Wilson Avenue, turned onto Indian Valley Road, and then walked down McClay Road. After climbing over a sagging section of barbed wired fence, I hiked up the grassy hillside. I stopped at a flat place beside a large rock, sat down to read my Bible, and pray. Within a few minutes I started thinking about my youngest brother, Robert.

I was hit with the idea that I had been a crummy big brother to Robert. I had never been there to help him through the trials of his life. Growing up, I had been consumed with my own pursuit of excitement and pleasure. I was asking the Lord to forgive me for my selfishness when I suddenly started crying. Within minutes I was sobbing deeply.

Afraid that I was losing control, I made myself stop crying. I remembered how I had cried when I had the drug-induced breakdown that led me to Napa State Hospital. I didn't want to have another breakdown.

Immediately, another thought came to me. "I'm a disciple of Jesus Christ. I'm not having a breakdown. I'm crying because I feel bad about what I have done in the past. This may be healing for my soul that I really need."

Then I was sobbing again. My thoughts about Robert had triggered the release of an emotional weight I was unaware I had been carrying. Looking back, I realize I was encountering the Holy Spirit. Just as Jesus promised in John 14:16, the Holy Spirit was comforting me. I was weeping and praying on that Novato hillside for a least an hour. Afterward, I got up and walked back to Solid Rock, feeling a lot lighter and somehow healthier.

I am not the kind of guy who cries easily; however, to this day, I often cry when the Holy Spirit moves on me.

The Holy Spirit knows when we are carrying pain in our hearts that needs to be released. Loving God with our whole heart means cooperating when the Holy Spirit touches our heart. If we are going to love deeply, we will also grieve deeply at times. The release of emotional pain through tears can help us process our pain in a healthy way.

The Prophecy

In the spring of 1971, Solid Rock hosted a weekly teaching series for eight weeks on the spiritual gifts listed in 1 Corinthians 12 and 14, and Romans 12. On the last night of the series, the teaching leaders and another man were going to pray over Ken, Cliff, and me. The three of us were involved in the ministry, and we had attended every class.

As we knelt beside the fireplace hearth, the Holy Spirit was present in a powerful way. The men circled around Ken and prayed for him first. They asked for the Lord to bless Ken and impart spiritual gifts to him. One of the men began to prophesy, "Ken, you are going to be a shepherd to the flock of God. You will feed God's people and care for them. They will go in and out and find good pasture under your care."

I got really excited as the men continued to pray. They moved over to where Cliff was kneeling. They began to speak blessings over Cliff as they prayed for him. It grew quiet for a moment, and then someone began to prophesy, "Cliff, you are called to be an evangelist. You will speak to multitudes and many will respond to Christ."

As I heard these prophecies, my heart began to beat faster. I could hardly wait for them to pray for me. I thought I spent more time seeking the Lord than either Ken or Cliff. If Ken was going to be a pastor and Cliff was going to be an evangelist, what was I going to be?

Gradually, the men gathered around me. My head was bowed on the hearth, and my heart pounded with anticipation. I felt the warm, heavy hands of the men resting on my shoulders. There were a couple of short prayers, and then they were silent. The moment had come. No one had ever prophesied to me before. I waited excitedly. Then one of the men spoke. "If you are faithful in the little things, I will give you responsibility over much."

There was silence again. In my heart I hoped for more, "Yes, yes, keep going!"

I was sure they were struggling to find the right words to

express the full extent of the blessing God had in store for me. Yet, while I waited for more promises, someone said, "Amen. Let's get some coffee." Our session ended, and they all moved away from me.

As we stood up, I saw that Ken and Cliff had huge smiles. They celebrated the promises they had been given by the Spirit. One was going to be a pastor and the other an evangelist. They looked over at me. "What did they say to you, Mark? Oh, yeah. Be faithful. That's good. Be faithful, brother. You can use that message." As they congratulated each other, I headed into my bedroom and shut the door. I kicked the wall in frustration. "I can't believe it. I got burned!"

It took me a while to settle down and think through the promise I had received. If I was faithful in the little things, God would make me responsible over much. The more I thought about it, the more it seemed like a challenge that I needed to accept. If God wanted me to be faithful, then I was going to be the most faithful disciple I could possibly be.

For the next few years, this prophecy became my motto. I drove kids to Bible studies, set up chairs at meetings, and handed out songbooks. I prayed, told people about Jesus, and did everything I possibly could to be a faithful disciple.

I did not know that this was just the first stage in my life where that prophecy would play an important role.

The Dream

One night at Solid Rock I had a dream that changed my life. In my dream, I saw people playing volleyball inside a gym. Some were White and others were Black. The ball went back and forth over the net as the game progressed. I thought I recognized the place as the gym at Terra Linda High School. Suddenly, a man with an angelic face appeared in the dream. He looked at me and instructed, "Be here tomorrow night at 7:30."

I woke up and felt the Lord had spoken to me. I contemplated the dream for several minutes. I concluded that an angel had appeared in my dream and I was supposed to go to the Terra Linda High gym at 7:30 P.M. However, because both Black and White people were in the gym, I thought the gym might be in Marin City, where more Black people lived. Terra Linda High School was primarily White.

I shared my dream with Malcolm. We agreed to go to Terra Linda High School at 7:30 that night. I had no clear idea who we were supposed to meet or what we were supposed to do. I assumed I was supposed to share the gospel with someone special, so we took some gospel tracts with us. We arrived at the school about 7:15. It looked deserted. By that time, all the teachers had headed home, and the school was closed.

Malcolm and I headed straight to the gym and found the doors locked. As we peered through the thick-glass front door, we could see that the gym was set up to host a school play. It looked like there might be a student or a janitor inside, but nobody responded when we knocked loudly on the door.

We wandered around the school and looked in the windows of empty classrooms. Being at my high school brought back all kinds of memories. I found myself wishing I had known the Lord in high school, because I had wasted a lot of time and destroyed many brain cells getting stoned. The longer we wandered around, the more I began to feel foolish. Maybe I misinterpreted the dream? We headed toward the parking lot to get back into the car. I wanted to go to Marin City before it got any later. Maybe there would be a gym in Marin City that fit my dream.

As we reached the edge of the parking lot, we saw a school bus approaching. We waited as it pulled up to the nearby curb. The bus door opened and the varsity baseball team began to emerge. We immediately went up to the players coming off the bus and offered them gospel tracts. Most of them took a tract, said "Thanks," and kept walking toward the locker room. I talked with a couple of the players for a few minutes and hoped the seeds we were sowing would produce some fruit.

The last person off the bus was Don Lucas, the varsity baseball coach. Don had been my football coach, as well as my varsity baseball coach when I played at Terra Linda.

I played three years of football, one year of basketball, and four years of baseball at Terra Linda High. We practiced three hours a day, every day, and traveled together to games. Those four years, I spent far more time with Don Lucas and the other coaches than I did with my own dad.

Coach Lucas greeted me warmly. He asked me what I was doing with my life. I told him that I had started following Jesus after getting myself into trouble with drugs. I explained that I was working in construction and living at the Solid Rock discipleship house in Novato.

I asked him if he knew the Lord. He immediately told me that he was a Christian. He also mentioned he had helped start a

Fellowship for Christian Athletes [FCA] group on campus.

Coach Lucas then followed the team, and Malcolm and I got into my truck and headed to Marin City. It had been nice to hear that Coach Lucas was following the Lord, but I didn't think that was the reason for my dream.

Malcolm and I got to Marin City in fifteen minutes. We found an open gym where a number of African Americans were playing basketball. We waited for an opportunity and then joined in some five-on-five, half-court games. Afterward, we walked around the gym and tried to talk to a few of the guys about the Lord. They listened politely but were not very responsive.

By then it was getting late. We headed back to the truck to leave and discovered that someone had stolen Malcolm's guitar out of the cab of the truck. Malcolm loved his guitar and took it everywhere he went. He was constantly playing worship songs to the Lord. We were both upset on the way home. Malcolm grieved because he lost his guitar. I was upset because it seemed like my powerful dream had not panned out as I had expected.

During the next two months, I learned I had made a hasty conclusion. That evening began a new phase in my life and ministry.

CHAPTER SIXTEEN

EXPANDING
OPPORTUNITIES
AND EXPERIENCES

Sharing My Testimony at High Schools

Within a week, Coach Lucas phoned and invited me to share my testimony with the Fellowship of Christian Athletes group at Terra Linda High. I went to the meeting and spoke to eight student athletes and two coaches.

They listened intently as I shared with them how I had started smoking marijuana and then had begun taking LSD at Terra Linda High School. I told them how fun it was at first, before I ended up in Napa State Hospital and became so depressed that I thought about killing myself.

They listened even more intently as I told them about the electroshock treatments and the confusion I went through before finding Christ. I shared how Jesus was healing my mind and how he had filled me with the Holy Spirit.

A few days later, the other coach who was at the FCA meeting called and asked if I would come to speak to the health education classes he taught. He wanted me to share my testimony with his students. I spent the whole day speaking to all five of his classes.

He was so excited about the students' responses that he told several other teachers about me. They invited me to speak at their history and health education classes.

Over the next few months, I had chances to preach the gospel to hundreds of students, most of whom never attended church. On one afternoon, the teachers opened up sliding doors, and three classes of students filled an expanded room while I spoke. Don Micheletti, the school newspaper editor, was present as I spoke to the three classes at once. Don wrote a full-page article about my testimony and soon began to follow the Lord.

The teachers at Terra Linda High School told teachers at San Rafael High about my story. In the following months, I spoke to classes at San Rafael High, Drake High, Redwood High, and Tam High. The students' responses to the gospel were so positive that we started weekly, lunchtime Bible studies at Terra Linda, San Rafael, and Redwood High Schools.

This continued for several years. I gave my testimony in the public high schools more times than I could count. The school principals were so glad that the students were getting an anti-drug message that they didn't care if I was sharing the gospel at the same time.

In addition, I started speaking to the health education classes about the dangers of abortion. In 1971, most abortions were illegal. I had many arguments with students when I started my messages by telling them abortion was wrong. I soon changed my approach. I told them the reality that a fetus's heartbeat could be detected eight weeks after conception. I explained how abortions were performed. Many students did not realize that fetuses were actually little babies living in their mothers' wombs. As they realized they had never been told the truth about the development of babies, they stopped arguing with me and we had many meaningful talks. The dream the Lord had given me that led me to Terra Linda High School bore wonderful fruit. It had opened up doors of ministry in the schools and changed my life. I went from being a carpenter recovering from a drug-damaged brain to a man eager to share the gospel of Christ everywhere I went.

Awesome Praise and Worship

In the summer of 1971, I went with several men from our ministry to a conference held at Bethany Bible College in the mountains near Santa Cruz. Most of those attending the conference stayed in the college dorm rooms or in nearby cabins. We didn't. To save money, we camped out under the redwood trees.

World Map Ministries sponsored the conference. The featured speaker was Bob Mumford, and the worship leader was Costa Dair from Elim Bible Institute in New York. The first night of the conference was unlike anything I had ever experienced.

Dancing in Praise to God

Costa was exuberant as he led us in praise and worship. After the first few songs, he started dancing on the stage. People throughout the auditorium also began dancing. I loved to dance before I started following the Lord, but I had never seen dancing like this before. Men and women were dancing joyfully before the Lord, rather than with each other.

After a few songs with dancing, Costa broke out in praise

and started singing in an unknown "tongue." Hundreds of people all through the congregation joined in a melodic chorus of different tongues. To me, their voices sounded like a choir of angels, each singing their own song to the Lord, yet all blending together in harmony.

I didn't know what to do, other than to watch the dancing and listen to the beautiful singing. That evening, the focus of prayer was for God to open the doors for the gospel to get into China. At that time, China was a completely closed-off communist country. An offering was taken to help fund missionaries going into China. I gave to the offering, even though the money I brought had to last the entire week of the conference.

We got back to our campsite late that night. The next morning we asked all the men to chip in money so we could buy groceries for the week. We found out one of the guys had been so moved by the call to give to China that he had put all the money he had brought with him into the offering. After he did this, we had to pay for his food all week. Fortunately, the Lord provided for us, and we all had plenty to eat.

On the second day of the conference, I started dancing along with everyone else. At first I was self-conscious about jumping up and down in place, but after a few minutes, I got caught up in a freedom of worship I had never experienced before. It was liberating to wholeheartedly dance without trying to impress anyone other than the Lord.

Singing in the Spirit

As the dancing quieted down, people began to sing in the

Spirit again. Once more, I felt like I was in the midst of a choir of heavenly angels. This time, I wanted more than anything to join in with the others. I knew I had the gift of tongues, but I had never been exposed to singing in the Spirit before. I started quietly speaking in tongues, but I struggled to sing in tongues.

After the meeting ended, I had a real breakthrough. During the lunch break, I found a secluded spot under the redwood trees and started singing quietly in tongues. I knelt among the majestic redwoods, and before long, I felt as though the cork came out of the bottle of my soul. Instead of a trickle of tongues, there was now a strong flow coming out of my soul through my mouth. The liberation I had felt earlier during the dancing was now happening in a similar way through this new kind of singing. By the time I rejoined the others at our camp, I was on a spiritual high.

At the meeting that night, I freely joined in the dancing and singing in the Spirit. I felt like I had been baptized in the Holy Spirit all over again. A new dimension of praise and worship opened up to me that I never knew was possible. At the end of that week, I returned home feeling like a transformed man.

I didn't want to lose the new freedom I had experienced at the missions conference. I began to incorporate singing in the Spirit, as well as prayer and Bible study, into the personal worship and devotion sessions that were now part of my daily routine.

It was important to me to find places where I could be alone for my devotions, since I didn't want to be interrupted or overheard when I was praying or singing with intensity. One afternoon, I went to the water-tank hill in Terra Linda where I had first experienced the presence of the Holy Spirit in prayer. I climbed to the top of the hill, sat down, and began to pray. I prayed with intensity and took time to speak in tongues as well. After a while, I began to feel the grace and peace that often accompanies the presence of the Holy Spirit. I started to sing in the Spirit. After a few minutes, I really began to cut loose with praise in tongues.

As my heart filled to overflowing with gratitude for the new life Jesus had given me, I stood up, lifted my arms, and shouted thanks to the Lord. Then, singing loudly in the Spirit, I started to skip down the steep path. I had skipped about forty yards when I heard a scream, "He's coming!" Two boys jumped out of a bush right beside the trail and scrambled, screaming down the hill as fast as they could run.

I stopped in my tracks. It took me a minute to realize what had happened. The boys had been on a hike up the hill when they had heard me praying and singing in the Spirit. Most likely they had never heard anything like the sounds I was making. So, curious, they had decided to sneak up on me and take a closer look. They had crept up through the trees and stopped at a big bush about fifty yards away from me. When suddenly I had stood up, raised my hands into the air, started singing in this strange language louder than ever, and started skipping right toward them. They must have thought they had discovered the mysterious Big Foot and now he was coming to kill them.

The Revival

One summer evening I was drawn to a large tent and a sign hung in the parking lot of the shopping center in Corte Madera along Highway 101: TRIPLE I C CRUSADE REVIVAL.

Marin County had never had a gospel crusade like this before. There was no history of tent meeting revivals in this wealthy, liberal, secular county. The tent was packed with people, 90 percent of whom were African American. Less than two percent of the population of Marin County was African American. Of the 600 students in my graduating class at Terra Linda High School, only three were African American. The people at the crusade were singing with great enthusiasm. The choir danced as they sang, and Fred Small, the pastor who organized the event, constantly wiped sweat off his brow with a white handkerchief as he shouted out the gospel with humor and power.

I was captivated by the love these folks had for the Lord. I was taken in by the many hugs they gave me before and after the revival service. And I felt truly blessed to meet Fred Small, a dynamic preacher of the Word.

I returned the next night and was blessed once again by their faith and love. After being a hippie for a couple of years and experiencing the love of that culture, it was very refreshing to experience love from these Black believers who did not know me or want anything other than that I would grow in my love for Jesus.

In my limited experience, people in predominantly Black churches give twice as many hugs and sing twice as loud as those in White churches. Their preachers are often more dynamic and their singers sing with more soul than typical White believers.

Following the second night of the revival, I was hitchhiking home when a young man named Bob Pangburn picked me up. We started talking and I found out that he also attended College of Marin. I invited him to one of Kent's Bible studies. Two months later he moved in with us at Solid Rock. Bob became my first real friend in the Jesus Movement. Bob and I shared lunches at school and a bedroom at Solid Rock. His faith and love have enriched my life ever since. Friends are a great source of joy.

CHAPTER SEVENTEEN

STARTING TO LEAD

One disadvantage of owning Trident Builders was the reality that every time we finished a construction project, we were out of work until we had a contract for another job. I tried to catch up on paperwork between jobs. When that was finished, I would go out and evangelize.

One of those evangelistic outreaches became another turning point in my life.

One summer day, Malcolm and I left Solid Rock and drove over Mount Tamalpais to Stinson Beach. We spent the afternoon going from one group of people on their beach blankets to the next. We would offer people tracts or Christian newspapers, and ask them if they knew Jesus was alive.

Not everyone welcomed us, but many people were eager to talk. I found it fascinating when people opened their hearts and allowed us to talk with them about some of their deepest feelings. Within minutes of meeting a person and handing them a tract, we were discussing the person's faith, life experiences, and families. We sowed many seeds of truth into people's hearts before heading home that afternoon.

On the way back, we stopped and picked up two young hitchhikers. We began talking about the Lord with these two high school boys as soon as they got into our car. They were both open to this. Half an hour later, we stopped to drop them off in Tiburon. Before they got out, I asked if they would be interested in asking Jesus Christ to be their Lord and Savior. Much to my amazement, both replied, "Yes." The four of us prayed together as the boys gave their lives to Christ. I was elated because they were the first people I had ever directly led to Jesus. I gave them my phone number and told them to give me a call if they ever wanted to get together and talk about the Lord.

A week or so later, one of the boys called. He asked if I would be willing to come and teach the Bible to him and some of his friends. I explained that I couldn't do it because I was just getting familiar with the Bible myself and felt unqualified to teach anyone else. I did tell them I would like to visit their meeting if they found someone to lead it.

My days of not teaching the Bible soon ended.

One evening at Kent's Bible study, Kai Adler came to the meeting. I knew Kai from Terra Linda High. Kai was a Canadian, whose parents emigrated from Norway to Canada at the end of World War II. They moved to the U.S. when Kai was young. Kai had started a Bible study at his parents' house in Lucas Valley. He invited me to come and give a teaching to the group. I felt like the Lord was challenging me, so I agreed to do it.

Leading My First Bible Study

On the night I gave the first Bible teaching of my life, Kai's living room was filled with Jesus people from Marin County. I don't know if anyone else remembers my message, but the lesson I taught was based on Mark 12:28–30. My theme was "Love God with your whole mind, heart, soul, and strength." I have tried to live by that theme ever since.

A few weeks later, Jim, one of the boys I had picked up hitchhiking from the beach, called again. This time he told me they had found a pastor who was teaching them the Bible. He invited me to come and visit the meeting.

I went to their Bible study at a home on a hill in Corte Madera. There were about ten high school students in the meeting, led by the pastor I met at the tent crusade, Fred Small. Everyone shared scripture and prayed at the meeting before Fred led us in a Bible study.

At the end of his teaching, Fred announced that this was the last week he could come to the meeting because of his responsibilities at his church. He suggested that I would be a good leader for the meeting.

The kids thought that sounded like a good idea. I agreed to give it a try, though I was nervous about the challenge of teaching each week. I prepared a lesson during the week and was too tense to eat dinner on most Tuesdays for the rest of the year.

After a few weeks, we moved the meetings to the fellowship hall of Westminster Presbyterian Church in Tiburon. Our group fluctuated from eight to fifteen students. We often prayed for the Lord to use us to reach many people and bring revival. We wanted a spiritual awakening that would result in people all over the world coming to know the Lord.

The meetings were going well until one night when nothing seemed to work. That Tuesday night, several kids brought friends to the meeting. It was the largest group we had ever had. We began to sing, but the singing was quieter than usual. When we began our prayer time, only one person besides me prayed aloud. I realized the kids were nervous about having their friends at the meeting. Nobody wanted to share anything when it was time to share testimonies and scripture.

I began my prepared message earlier than usual. My tongue felt thick and began to stick to the roof of my mouth as I spoke. Every word seemed strained and forced. I felt like the Spirit must be telling me to change topics. I did a quick change of topic and told everyone to turn to a different Bible passage. That didn't help.

I continued to struggle as I looked into the faces of the kids who wanted so desperately to have the friends they brought meet Christ. After a couple of minutes, I made another switch. I shut my Bible and just started sharing my testimony. Perplexed looks crossed several of their faces as I continued. Everything was strained that night. I felt like a failure as we drove home.

The next Tuesday night we were down to a dozen or so in attendance. We all knew what had happened, but we didn't discuss it. We weren't ready to handle the answers to the prayers we had been praying. We thought we had missed our chance for a revival, but we tried to stay faithful.

The meetings started to grow after the first year. The room became packed each week with kids sitting on the floor for the worship, prayer, sharing, and teaching times. I never considered it a youth group, but most of the kids I taught were too young to drive. I picked many of them up in my truck before the meeting. One Tuesday night we set a record with twenty-three of us packed into my Ford pickup, which had a camper shell. After that, we found other kids to drive. I gave them gas money if they needed it.

At the end of each meeting, I would invite them to give their lives to Christ. Each week, young men and women would raise their hands to indicate that they were making a first-time decision to become disciples of Christ.

At the time, I thought that must happen whenever someone preached the gospel. I know now the response we were getting was not because I was such a great Bible teacher; rather, we were part of a spiritual awakening—the Jesus Movement.

I had no plans to ever become a pastor or minister. I had no expectations that my teaching would have great long-term impact. I simply taught the Bible to kids who were hungry to learn.

As time went by, I came to love these young disciples deeply. I wanted to help guide them into the most fruitful lives possible. I continued to lead those meetings until the end of 1973. Many years later, I had a completely different take on the years I spent teaching those kids about Christ. What had seemed like a little ministry, with only minimal impact, was actually a launching pad for missionaries and fruitful disciples. I have had more contact with some of the girls in the group than the guys, so I'll mention three of them whom our churches have helped to support over the years.

Marilyn Mergens was the younger sister of Jim, the boy I had picked up hitchhiking from Stinson Beach. She started following Christ in that Bible study when she was in the seventh grade. Marilyn was so shy when she first showed up that she often wouldn't even answer a direct question when I spoke with her. As the Lord transformed her, Marilyn became one of the worship leaders in our

Bible study. She ended up marrying Jerry Farnick after graduating from college. They became missionaries to Czechoslovakia in the early 1980s and have remained in the Czech Republic, serving the Lord with their three children.

Pam Hawkins started attending our Bible study when she was a freshman at Redwood High School. Pam had a spirit of divination when I first met her. We prayed for Pam, and she went through a powerful deliverance and became a committed disciple of Christ. After graduating from college, Pam and her husband, Dan Clancy, moved to Turkey, where they were missionaries with their four children for many years.

Donna Long was a key leader in our Bible study at Terra Linda High School. Donna and Marilyn sang together at weddings and church services for several years. After graduating from college, Donna married Yale Kushner, a Jewish believer. Donna and Yale have served full time in missions with Campus Crusade for Christ [Cru] since the early 1980s. They served for years reaching out to Muslims in Israel and France. They then spent years training leaders for ministry at the Cru headquarters in Orlando.

We had prayed for the Lord to use us to touch the world. We had expected those prayers to be answered within days of our petitions reaching heaven. Looking back, I see how God used our little group to impact the world. His timing took longer than we had imagined, but His grace has given each of our lives more impact than we had expected.

Leadership and Bookstores

Kent Philpott created a nonprofit corporation for our discipleship houses and Bible studies called House Ministries. He was our pastor and provided leadership, along with a team of elders, none of whom was older than thirty.

In late 1971, I was added to the leadership team. We met on Saturday afternoons in Petaluma, before our evening Bible study held at the Church of God. I had been eager to join the leadership team; however, I soon discovered the leadership meetings were more focused on dealing with difficult earthly problems than uplifting spiritual discussions. We had disagreements, limited finances, and the pressure of overseeing hundreds of young people involved in our growing ministry.

A young Jewish man named Barry accepted the Lord and moved into one of our discipleship houses. He heard we were hoping to purchase a farm in Petaluma for a discipleship house and gave our ministry $3,000. That money was a windfall to us, but it was not enough to enable us to buy the farm. A vigorous discussion ensued in our leadership meeting about whether to return the money to him.

Our discussion turned to the lack of bookstores anywhere in Marin County that sold Christian books, Bibles, and music. Our converts needed new Bibles, and we all read Christian books. A Catholic store in San Rafael had gone out of business the year before. All this led us to believe that we should start a good Christian bookstore. A business consultant told us that it would take about $20,000 for first and last month's rent, shelves, insurance, books, music, and Sunday school and church supplies. We found a location, but all we had was the $3,000 from Barry. We decided to go for it.

In late 1971, we opened The Christian General Store on the

Miracle Mile in San Rafael. Betty Kenner was our first store manager. Betty was the mother of Kristina, the beautiful, dark-haired girl I had met at a Bible study, who I was now dating. After Betty had separated from Kristina's dad, she had moved into a women's discipleship house in San Rafael. Betty had the management skills we needed. She was also willing to work for $400 a month, just enough to pay her share of the food and rent at the house, with a little left for personal expenses. Several volunteers helped Betty.

The Christian General Store provided a central point for our ministries, as well as a gathering place for many believers in Marin. The store did well from the start. We put the profits back into the business to build up the inventory, adding more books, Bibles, and music.

People would wander into the store and receive prayer, ministry, and directions to good local churches. This resulted in Betty becoming a spiritual mother to many young people in Marin. She provided me with books to help me grow in Christ. I became one of Betty's best customers, buying many copies of books like *The Hiding Place* and *Deliver Us from Evil* to give to my friends.

Focusing on Family

In November of that year, I moved out of Solid Rock and back in with my mom and siblings in Terra Linda. By this time, I had a good spiritual foundation. My parents had divorced, and I wanted to help support our family. I had income from construction work, so I paid my mom rent and helped around the house. More than anything, I wanted to lead my family to Christ. That proved to be a challenge, but my prayers were eventually answered.

After a full day on the job, Mom had to come home and cook, clean, and do everything for the kids. I took time with the Lord in the mornings, led Trident Builders, and then came home and cooked dinner most nights. It took two hours for me to prepare meat, potatoes, and salad for the nine of us.

I felt guilty about the way I had ordered my younger siblings around when we were younger. I was hoping this season would enable me to serve my family by example and lead them to Christ.

My four younger sisters were beautiful girls and at stages in life where they needed attention from their dad. They also needed discipline because they were often fighting. My mom, wisely, would not let me discipline my sisters. To try and keep order in the house, I did some yelling and threatening along with my serving. However, I was not mature enough to give my sisters the love and attention they really needed.

My brother, Robert, was the first one who responded to the Lord and started coming to Bible studies with me. Robert came home from his birth at the hospital when I had just turned six years old. He was the fifth Buckley child. Robert began to follow Christ and joined me at Bible studies when he was a high school freshman. He became a committed believer right away.

One day, when he was walking through San Rafael, a group of Hells Angels pulled in to a gas station on their motorcycles in front of him. Robert felt like the Lord wanted him to share his faith, so he went up to the bikers as they were filling their gas tanks. He began to talk with them about Jesus. Robert was like a lamb sharing the gospel with a pack of wolves. Fortunately, the wolves were so impressed by his courage they were receptive to his message about Jesus.

    As the year ended, the Jesus Movement was in full swing. Because so many young people were sharing their faith boldly, the gospel was spreading throughout the country. It didn't take much maturity to become a leader in the Jesus Movement. Those who knew the Scriptures and stayed faithful for a couple of years had opportunities to become leaders. I had grown in my walk with God and now had many opportunities for ministry.

CHAPTER EIGHTEEN

LEARNING THROUGH EXPERIENCE

A Painful Experience

By 1972, my confidence in the Lord had grown. Unfortunately, my wisdom had not caught up to my boldness.

One weeknight, I dropped by the priest's house at St. Isabella's, the Catholic church in Terra Linda where I grew up. An evening Bible study with one of the parish priests was just starting up. I was late, but a lady who worked for the priests greeted me warmly at the door. She led me into the living room where eight people were sitting. The priest welcomed me, and after I introduced myself, he explained that their discussion of the Gospel of Mark was just getting started.

I was about to learn the hard way why the Apostle Paul said that speaking in tongues in church should always be followed by an interpretation.

As the priest began to explain some of the differences between the gospels of Matthew, Mark, Luke, and John, he stated that the gospels cannot be taken literally because of their textual differences. I was stunned. I didn't want to disagree with him in front of the others and struggled to contain myself.

I had never met the priest before, and we were in his home, with people who were looking to him for guidance. I listened in silence for a few more minutes until he mentioned another reason why the Bible cannot be trusted historically. While the others in the room just sat and listened attentively, my heart was beating rapidly. I finally spoke up, "I think you can definitely take the New Testament literally. The Bible is as true today as it was when it was written."

"Excuse me. No scholars take the Bible literally anymore. It must be interpreted in its context. How would you know anyway?" the priest asked curtly.

I looked at him and responded, "I know the things the Bible says are true. God is still giving gifts of the Spirit to people today."

"I don't think that has been happening for the last 2,000 years," he smirked.

My heart was pounding. I didn't want to argue, but I felt I had to defend the Lord and give these people a chance to know the truth. "Well, I know that speaking in tongues is still valid today."

"How can you prove that?" he asked sarcastically.

With his challenge, and the eyes of the others fixed upon me, I took the bait and began to speak boldly in tongues. After about a minute of me speaking loudly in tongues, the priest recovered from his stunned shock. He stood up quickly, grabbed me by the arm, and pulled me toward the front door like an angry principal leading a rebellious child. He opened the door, pushed me out and declared, "Don't ever come back around here again!"

I walked home feeling like a failure. I felt badly that I had used speaking in tongues to try to demonstrate the truth of the

Bible. The gifts of the Spirit are precious, and we should not try to prove the truth of the Bible by using these gifts in ways the Bible prohibits. 1 Corinthians 12–14 teaches tongues should be used to edify an individual or the church, and tongues should have an interpretation when used in a public setting.

I also learned that there is no way to convince someone of the veracity of speaking in tongues if the person does not believe the Bible is trustworthy and true in the first place.

Years later, I would tell this story publicly for the first time. That situation ended with even more drama than the night at the priest's house.

Special People and Events in 1972

In the spring of 1972, I hitchhiked from Marin County down to Long Beach with Bern Powers. We were headed to a teaching conference featuring Bob Mumford, Derek Prince, Don Basham, and The Second Chapter of Acts, a singing group led by Annie Herring. We caught one ride after another and arrived in time for the first night's dynamic teaching and worship session.

At the end of the meeting, we exited the arena, along with several thousand other believers. We stood outside with our backpacks and began looking for someone who might offer us a place to stay for the night.

Meeting Frank O'Neil

We spotted a friendly-looking guy who wore his brown hair in a ponytail. I asked him if he knew where we could "crash" for the night. He told us his name was Frank and we could stay with him and his friend at an apartment they were using. On the drive to the apartment, we got to know Frank O'Neil as we sang worship songs and shared stories about how God had saved each of us. Bern and I slept comfortably on the rug in the apartment the next two nights. By the end of the conference, we had learned that Frank lived on a farm with his family in Santa Cruz. He had started a Jesus people ministry there, and he invited Bern and me to visit them.

Two weeks later, we took my truck and drove to Santa Cruz to stay with Frank, his beautiful wife, Patty, and their three young daughters. They had a nice house and several animals on their small, hillside farm. Their two goats were named Goodness and Mercy, from Psalm 23. They lived up to their names by following us everywhere we went around the farm.

Frank and Patty introduced us to several of their friends. Danny Lehmann was one of the young leaders in their ministry who would have a big impact on my life in the years to come.

An Encounter in Dallas

In the summer of 1972, I went with several of the Jews for Jesus to Explo '72 in Dallas, Texas. More than 40,000 young people from around the nation came to this training event sponsored by Campus Crusade for Christ.

Moishe Rosen, founder of Jews for Jesus, brought several of us to the conference to hand out tracts and prepare promotional materials to be presented to those attending the conference. He brought huge stacks of *Christian LIFE Magazine* to be included in the materials being distributed.

The cover of *Christian LIFE* featured a dark-haired Jewish girl who was a part of their ministry. As I sorted through the stack of magazines, placing one in each of the batches of materials, I became captivated by the piercing eyes and smooth complexion of the girl on the cover. I had no idea I would soon be meeting her. Moishe was a genius at maximizing the impact of the Jews for Jesus. Sunday morning, before the conference began, he posted us in front of the doors of First Baptist Church in Dallas, one of the biggest churches in America. Billy Graham was the morning's scheduled preacher.

I was assigned a place at one of the side entrances to the church and given a stack of Jews for Jesus evangelism "broadsides" to hand to those who entered. Broadsides are simple cartoons with a gospel message on 8.5" x 11" paper, folded to create a three-sided pamphlet. The message on this broadside read, "It doesn't matter if you are rich or poor, hippie or straight, Black, Brown or White . . . you must be born again."

As the time came for the service to begin, the crush of people pouring into the church slowed down. I noticed some men in black suits emerging from a building across the street. They looked like Secret Service agents. They walked quickly toward me.

I held back offering them a tract, just in case they were with the church. I assumed we didn't have permission to do what we were doing. Then I recognized Billy Graham among the group. My heart started pounding. As he approached, I reached out and offered him a broadside. "Here is something you might enjoy, Mr. Graham. God bless you," I blurted quickly.

Billy paused, took the tract, and thanked me as he continued to walk into the sanctuary. I was excited I had a chance to meet the world's most famous evangelist. There were no more people arriving, so I walked around to the front of the huge building. I met up with Bruce, one of the Jews for Jesus, who had been posted at the main entrance. We walked into the sanctuary, which was packed with thousands of worshipers, and squeezed into a pew in the back.

After hymns, prayers, a greeting, an offering, and a song sung by a soloist, Billy got up to speak. He smiled and his voice boomed over the microphone as he greeted the congregation. He began to tell stories about meeting the Queen of England and sharing the gospel around the world. Toward the end of his message he declared, "It doesn't matter if you are rich or poor, hippie or straight, Black, Brown, or White . . . you must be born again!"

Billy Graham was quoting directly from the broadside I had given him! At any minute I expected him to say, "And I would now like the young man who gave me the tract with this great line to please come and join me on the stage." He didn't say that or anything like it, but at least I knew that he had read the broadside, and through him, it had an impact on the First Baptist Church.

Participating in Explo '72

Explo '72 was the largest and best-organized event I had ever attended. More than 40,000 people gathered in the Cotton Bowl each night of the conference. We sang songs of praise that rocked the stadium. We listened to Bill Bright, the founder of Cru, and other speakers who were filled with wisdom and insight. Each day, we attended breakout sessions where we received instruction on evangelism, Bible study, and the Spirit-filled life. One afternoon, thousands of us did door-to-door evangelism throughout Dallas. The conference concluded with an outdoor festival attended by more than 200,000 people who gathered on a huge grassy area. Johnny Cash and Kris Kristofferson sang, and Billy Graham preached. It was the height of the Jesus Movement in America, and it seemed like we would win the world for Christ.

I left inspired and eager to keep sharing my faith.

Praying for My Friend's Mom

After Explo '72, the Jews for Jesus headed back to California without me. I took a Greyhound bus to Nashville, to visit Roger Allan, my friend from Solid Rock. Roger had only lived at Solid Rock for a few months, but I was impressed by his faith. One time, he hitchhiked from Nashville to Novato with only six dollars in his pocket. He came all that way just to spend a few days with us and then hitchhiked back home.

Roger was now living with his mother. We spent several hours talking about the Lord during the two days I stayed with them. The second night, Roger's mom asked me to pray for her. I don't remember the exact problem she told me she was having, but I remember thinking that she seemed to need deliverance from obsessive fear.

I prayed a simple prayer commanding every demonic spirit that was tormenting her to leave her in Jesus' name. As soon as I commanded the demons to leave, her body started to shake and she released a bloodcurdling scream.

Within an hour, we were done praying, and she seemed to be at peace.

This was a special encounter for me. Her experience was like several I had witnessed during deliverance sessions in California. Yet, she had no knowledge of what we had been doing in our deliverance ministry in California. I had not coached her or told her what might happen; yet, when Mrs. Allan was delivered from demonic spirits, she reacted almost identically to others who were 2,000 miles away. It reaffirmed for me the validity and importance of deliverance ministry.

Hitchhiking to New York

From Nashville, I began to hitchhike to Rome in upstate New York to spend some time with my friend Bob Pangburn before heading home. It took several days to get there. First, I traveled east from Nashville to North Carolina. There, I found myself on a lonely freeway on-ramp at sunset with no cars entering the freeway. As it grew darker, I started praying, asking the Lord to provide a ride for me. It was common for me to pray as I waited for rides. I often asked the Lord to send along a person He wanted to bless. Since no cars were coming, I walked down the on-ramp onto the shoulder of the freeway. I knew this was illegal, but I didn't want to spend the night in the nearby field.

A Weird Driver

Even the freeway traffic was sparse that evening, but eventually an old car slowed and the driver pulled onto the shoulder a hundred yards past me. I saw the driver trying to back up toward me, so I joyfully put on my backpack and jogged up to the car. I opened the car door and saw a man in an old shirt and jeans. I thanked him for stopping and told him I was heading for New York. He didn't say anything as I put my backpack in his back seat and sat down in the front seat next to him.

I had started hitchhiking in junior high school. I always went out of my way to be friendly and talk with whoever picked me up. A little friendliness goes a long way when you are a hitchhiker. I had learned that a driver who liked me would sometimes go out of his way to take me where I needed to go. I tried being friendly to this man as we drove, but I realized quickly something was wrong.

He would not respond to my questions or comments, so I tried to be quiet and polite. I was thankful to be driving toward New York and not having to sleep in the bushes. After a while, the guy began to twitch and look behind him. "Who are you signaling," he asked me.

"What?"

"Who are you signaling? I saw you signal someone!"

"I wasn't signaling anyone. I don't even know anyone around here."

"I saw you scratch your ear. I know you were signaling someone! Are you with the CIA?"

"I don't know anyone in the CIA. Honestly, I don't, or I wouldn't be out here hitchhiking."

For a minute I had hoped he might be joking, but my experiences at Napa State Hospital had taught me that paranoid people do not joke around. They can be serious . . . and seriously crazy.

This fellow kept looking back over his shoulder, trying to see who I was signaling. Then he would stare at me while he was driving sixty miles an hour down the freeway. I looked straight ahead, hoping he would believe me, keep his eyes on the road, and drop the subject. This was a dangerous situation and I didn't like my alternatives. We were driving along a deserted stretch of freeway and it was pitch-dark outside.

He didn't calm down. He kept staring at me while I tried to sit motionless, giving him no reason to suspect me of being his enemy. Finally, I saw a highway sign for a café and a gas station as we approached a small town. I wanted to get out of his car as fast as possible.

I told him, "This is as far as I'm going. Thanks very much for the ride. You can let me out right here, if you don't mind."

Fortunately, with another couple of glances over his shoulder, he pulled over and let me out. It was nighttime, on the edge of nowhere. I was shaking with adrenaline but thankful to be out of his car. The café and the gas station were closed. I walked down the road and found some small trees surrounded by bushes. I went into the bushes and unrolled my sleeping bag for the night.

I slept through the night and woke up at first light. Seeing a couple of cars parked in front of the café, I went in and ordered pancakes and coffee. After breakfast, I walked through the town and began to hitchhike on the on-ramp leading back to the freeway. One of the first cars to come by stopped, and I got a ride toward Virginia.

A Receptive Driver

On the way, the driver opened his heart to me and shared some of the struggles in his life. He listened quietly as I shared with him the good news that Jesus is alive. When he pulled over to drop me off a couple hours later, I prayed with him to ask Jesus to come into his heart and be his Savior.

I was filled with joy as I resumed the trip north. The next ride took me through the Shenandoah Valley of Virginia. The tall mountains covered with big green trees, along with pastures, farms, and barns, looked like settings for Norman Rockwell paintings.

The man who drove me through this majestic valley was also very open to Christ. We drove all the way to lower New York, talking the whole time. At the end of my ride with him, he also prayed with me to give his life to Jesus.

I have hitchhiked thousands of miles and received hundreds of rides, but this was the only time I have ever been able to lead two different drivers to Christ, one after the other. I realized God had used the crazy driver from the night before to get me right where He wanted me.

However, the next day was not as successful. It was Sunday morning, and there weren't many cars on the road. So, I started to walk through a small town. I saw a church with a crowded parking lot. As I stopped to rest, the church doors opened, and people started coming out of the sanctuary into the parking lot. I was relieved, thinking I would be able to catch a ride with some believers at any moment.

I put down my backpack, smiled, and extended my arm with my thumb raised in the politest way possible. However, one by one, the cars drove past me. I could understand how a family whose car was filled with kids would drive by without picking me up, but I had a harder time understanding why couples, or men without any passengers, would not stop. I started praying the Lord would bless whoever stopped to pick me up; yet, nobody stopped.

After a while the church parking lot was empty, so I started walking again. I wondered what the pastor had preached about that morning. How could an entire congregation of people who are supposed to love Jesus Christ and love their neighbors drive right past a brother in need?

I finally made it to Rome, New York, and spent several days with my friend Bob Pangburn. As I related earlier, Bob and I had become friends when he picked me up hitchhiking in Corte Madera. We both attended College of Marin and moved into Solid Rock together in 1971. Bob was a potter and a beekeeper who loved the Lord. He made beautiful honey pots and filled them with honey from his bees. These made great gifts, which he sold throughout upstate New York. After a week of fellowship with Bob, I flew home to California.

A Request

Returning home, I made my relationship with the Lord my priority. I tried to make time each day for Bible study and prayer. I found privacy in the hills above Terra Linda, which were preserved as open space for the community.

One summer morning, I hiked to a sloping spot on a hillside covered with long wild grasses. I could see San Pablo Bay to the east and Highway 101 snaking south toward San Francisco. I climbed over the barbed-wire fence that had once kept the dairy cows from wandering. I lay down to seek the Lord. As I called upon the Lord, I had an intense encounter with the Holy Spirit.

I had spent as much or more time studying the Old Testament as I had the New Testament, and I had recently read the book of Deuteronomy. I felt like the Lord was saying to me, "I am the God of Moses." I had my head bowed and said nothing for several minutes, because the Lord's presence was powerful and personal.

At the same time, I wanted to make sure I wasn't going crazy. Ever since my days in Napa State Hospital I had been insecure about my sanity. So, I decided to ask God for a sign, which is something I had never done before or since: "Lord, if You really are the God of Moses, I need to be sure. I would like You to remove this fence."

It was inconvenient to have to climb over the barbed-wire fence to my prayer spot every time I came to this hillside; however, I didn't pray for the fence to be removed because of inconvenience.

Instead, I felt the need to confirm that I was talking with the living God and not having spiritual delusions. I hoped I wasn't testing God, though I was insecure about that as well.

Soon afterward, I climbed back over the fence and headed down the hill to get ready for the rest of my day. It would be several years before I thought about that encounter again.

Danny Lehmann

One day in the fall, I received a call from Frank O'Neil, inviting me to come back to Santa Cruz. He had heard about the Bible studies I was leading in the high schools in Marin and wanted to start similar ministries at schools in Santa Cruz.

A week later, I met with several of the leaders of Frank's ministry. The point man for their evangelism outreach was a zealous young believer named Danny Lehmann.

Danny reminded me of a cartoon character from a gospel tract. He had sun-bleached hair, bright blue eyes, and a perpetual grin. Until he met Frank and some of his friends, Danny had been a surfer who enjoyed getting stoned. They shared Christ with Danny and brought him to their Bible studies.

After giving his life to Christ, Danny began leading others to the Lord almost every day. He worked as a concrete finisher to make money, but his passion was sharing Jesus and making disciples.

Danny was eager to hear how God had given me a dream and supernaturally opened the doors for our ministry in the Marin County high schools. I shared with him everything I had learned about finding favor with school administrators and impacting high school students. I had no idea at the time how much the friendship we formed would affect my life in the years to come.

Restitution

Bill Gothard was a Bible teacher who led a seminar called "Basic Youth Conflicts." Once a year during the 1970s, he came to the Cow Palace in San Francisco and held a five-day seminar attended by thousands of people. Bill spoke in a calm, straightforward manner, but he was able to keep our complete attention with his insights and the power of the Holy Spirit.

One of the teachings he emphasized in the seminar was restitution. After attending his seminar for the second time, I started my own journey of restitution. I wanted to be right with God in every way.

My first stop was Stan's Sporting Goods in San Rafael. In

my junior year of high school, I had wanted to buy snow skis, so I wouldn't have to rent them every time I went skiing. One afternoon, I walked into Stan's with two buddies and started looking at skis. The store was busy with customers. Without planning it in advance, I selected a pair of long black skis, put them over my shoulder and starting walking toward the cash register near the front door. I noticed that the man working the counter had stepped away to help another customer. So, I just kept walking with my buddies past the counter and out the door. We got in the car and drove away, laughing about the brazen heist.

After hearing Bill Gothard's teaching two years in a row, I felt I had to make restitution for those skis. I felt anxious as I drove to the store. I had brought my checkbook and was rehearsing what I would do when I arrived. I planned to confess to stealing the skis, ask the owner's forgiveness, and give him a check for $150, the price tag on the skis five years earlier.

I went to the store and found it had changed its name to Oshman's Sporting Goods. When I asked to speak with the owner, I was told to go to their corporate headquarters in an industrial park across the highway from Terra Linda.

When I arrived at the one-story brown office building, I asked a man walking past me if he could point me to the Oshman's office. He directed me around a corner. Inside the Oshman's office, a receptionist sat behind a desk. When she asked why I wanted to speak with the owner, my heart started beating faster. I told her I had become a Christian and I was there to ask forgiveness and pay for something I had stolen.

The receptionist picked up her phone, spoke to someone, and

asked me to wait for a few minutes. Then she left the room. When she returned, she led me down a corridor to where a secretary sat. The secretary asked how she could help me. I told her the same story I had told the receptionist. I felt like I was being examined a second time in a doctor's office for an embarrassing condition.

She nodded and picked up the phone and placed a call. She then led me toward another office, knocked on the door and opened it. There behind the desk sat the same man I had seen in the parking lot who had directed me toward their offices.

He seemed stern and reserved until I explained to him that I had come to ask forgiveness and make restitution for stealing skis from his store five years earlier. As I told him what I had done, his countenance began to soften. He started asking me questions about what had motivated me to come and make restitution. He wanted to know about the ministry I was involved in, and he asked me about my faith.

He then told me that in all his years of retail experience, no one had ever come to him to ask for forgiveness and make restitution for stealing. He refused to take my check. Instead, he requested permission to tell my story to his employees. He also asked if I knew any other young people like me he could hire.

I left his office stunned. I was amazed at the way God opened the heart of a sporting goods store owner because I had obeyed the prompting of the Holy Spirit. Blacky Smith needed a job, so I suggested he call the Oshman's office and tell them he was with our ministry. Blacky was hired to do their landscape work immediately.

This experience encouraged me to keep going through my restitution list.

A couple of weeks later, I went to Scotty's Market. I had worked at Scotty's for two years while attending Terra Linda High School. In those days I went to school Monday through Friday from 8:30 A.M. to 3:00 P.M. Classes were followed by baseball or football practice Monday through Friday from 3:30 to 5:30 P.M. I worked at Scotty's from 6:00 to 9:00 P.M. Monday, Wednesday, and Friday, and all day Saturday.

I got hungry on the days I had to work. One day while stocking the refrigerated shelves inside the dairy refrigerator, I drank a canned chocolate milkshake. I knew it was against store policy to eat on the job, so I didn't tell anyone or pay for the drink. It tasted so good I drank another one the next time I had refrigerator-stocking duty. I soon graduated to drinking a cold Mountain Dew as well. By the time I walked up the back steps toward the office to make restitution to Joe Messina, the owner of Scotty's Market, I calculated that I owed him at least a couple hundred dollars for stolen drinks.

I was ashamed to talk with Mr. Messina because he was my dad's friend. My dad had asked him to hire me when I was fifteen years old. Joe gave me my first real job, other than my paper route and lawnmowing. Every Christmas, he gave each employee a bonus check equal to two weeks pay. I was only making $2.02 an hour, but when gas cost only 25¢ a gallon and a movie ticket was 50¢, it was not a bad wage for a kid my age.

When I appeared at Mr. Messina's office door, he invited me to come in and sit down. I sat in a chair by his desk and looked through the window he had installed to keep an eye on the store below. "What can I do for you, Mark?" he asked.

I told him I had come to ask his forgiveness and make

restitution for stealing drinks during the last year of my employment at Scotty's. I showed him a check made out to Scotty's Market for $250, which I thought would cover the value of the beverages I had taken.

When I had finished, Mr. Messina looked me in the eye and revealed, "We knew you were doing that, Mark." His comment caught me off guard. I was embarrassed that Mr. Messina knew all along that I had been an employee he couldn't trust.

When I held out my check to him, he refused to take it. Instead, he pointed to a pile of boxes in the corner of his office. "Can you use some food for your ministry?" he asked. "We can't sell damaged packages."

I drove away in my truck with four boxes filled with slightly dented cans and partially torn packages of food for Solid Rock.

My conscience was lighter as I contemplated a spiritual reality. When the Lord gives us an assignment and we obey Him, amazing things can happen. Instead of living with guilt and shame, I had been forgiven and was being blessed.

Church of the Open Door

Throughout 1972, I worked closely with Kent Philpott and Ken Sanders leading our ministry and teaching Bible studies. It was a time of growth and change. One of the biggest changes occurred in August because Mike Riley and Roger Hoffman had been attending our Bible studies. Both were charismatic Christians who believed spiritual gifts are as important today as they were in the first century. They were best friends from Chico. They had graduated from Chico State and were active in the Neighborhood

Church. After graduation, they started attending Golden Gate Seminary, where they got to know Kent.

Mike and Roger were mature believers and soon became part of our leadership team. They brought another friend from the seminary named Bob Hymers to our meetings. Bob had been saved in the First Chinese Baptist Church in Los Angeles. He had developed a dynamic gift for preaching by leading the junior high class there for many years. Bob said, "If you can keep the attention of junior high kids, you can preach to anyone."

Bob, Mike, and Roger saw all the young people coming to our Bible studies. They felt called to start a church to help these young disciples grow in Christ. Kent, Ken Sanders, and I felt the time was not right for us to start a church, but we gave them our blessing to invite people from our ministry to join them.

Their new church was called Church of the Open Door. Their first meetings were held in the living room of Lloyd and Jan Dow in Mill Valley in August 1972. Bob chose the name because he admired the Church of the Open Door in Los Angeles and its pastor, J. Vernon McGee. They soon moved into Scout Hall in Mill Valley with thirty people, giving birth to the first of what developed into several Open Door churches.

Sunday Night Services

Kent, Ken, and I soon changed our mind about starting a church. Six months later, in early 1973, we decided to start Sunday night services at the Lucas Valley Community Church. We invited anyone coming to our Bible studies to join us.

Kent and I shared leadership responsibilities. On the week

Kent preached, I would lead the worship service. The following week, I would preach, and he would lead worship. My singing wasn't very good. Fortunately, after a few weeks, Tom Wise, a gifted singer, began to attend the services and soon began to lead us in worship.

Tom had been a Mormon missionary working in Mexico when his brother Randy was killed in a car accident. When Tom returned to California to attend the memorial service, the Lord touched his heart. Tom's Presbyterian parents had been praying for him ever since he joined the Mormon Church in college. Tom headed back to Mexico to resume his mission. He got as far as Los Angeles, but he was troubled in his soul. After some spiritual wrestling, he decided to turn around and go back to his parents' home in Novato. Tom went to Kent for counseling. His eyes were opened to the truth that everyone who believes Jesus Christ is Lord is a part of the body of Christ. Tom soon became one of my best friends in ministry.

As more people committed their lives to Christ, our Sunday night services flourished. One Sunday evening, two young men with long hair came up to the front of the sanctuary after my sermon. Greg Fugate and Greg Straw had recently started following the Lord and wanted to introduce themselves.

Many people would come and go through our ministry in those days. I remember thinking I would probably never see these Gregs again. I'm not a prophet. They both joined our church and became fruitful leaders. It's been more than forty-seven years, and we are friends to this day.

PART FIVE

NEW BEGINNINGS

CHAPTER NINETEEN

KRISTINA

Getting to Know Kristina

Several of the guys involved in our ministry lived together in a discipleship house in Petaluma called Berachah House.

One Saturday evening, I attended a Bible study there. As we prayed at the close of the meeting, everyone was standing in a big circle holding hands. I became distracted by the warm hand of the girl next to me. Her name was Kristina, and she had intrigued me from the first time I laid eyes on her. I didn't know she was just seventeen years old. Her mother, Betty, managed our Christian General Store in San Rafael.

I tried not to focus on her because I knew she was engaged to my friend Randy, who was an evangelist.

Randy and I would go out on the streets and to parks to hand out gospel tracts and talk with people about Jesus. One afternoon, I went to pick up Randy at Kristina's house. I saw Kristina working on the engine of her car. I was impressed by a girl who could fix her own car. Also, she looked beautiful in overalls. Her confident smile, deep hazel eyes, and great figure added to her allure.

Though she and Randy were engaged, and Randy was my friend, Kristina was very friendly with me. Sometime later, Kristina came to Solid Rock to spend the weekend with her friend Judy, who was living with us. That Sunday, after visiting one of the nearby churches, several of us went on a picnic. As we sat on one of the brown rolling hills in Novato, I started talking with Kristina.

She told me she and Randy had broken off their engagement. I wasn't sad for my friend Randy. I realized his loss gave me a great opportunity. Kristina captivated me with her love for God and her beauty. I was twenty-one, though I felt a lot older. Kristina was seventeen, and as smart and as mature as any girl I knew.

On our first official date, we attended a service at the Church of God in Marin City. This African-American congregation was led by Pastor Fred Small, whom I first met when I attended the revival his church had sponsored. I felt Kristina would like Fred's church if she was the kind of girl I thought she was.

Ours were the only White faces in the congregation, but the love of the people made us feel very welcome. Their worship music was inspiring, and Fred's message touched our hearts.

When I dropped Kristina off at her house after that evening service, she gave me a quick kiss on the cheek. That sealed the deal as far as I was concerned. In the following days, we started going out every chance we got.

When I would take Kristina to my construction sites, she was always interested in what we were building. Her dad, Charles Kenner, was working in Puerto Rico for Bechtel, the world's largest construction company at the time. He had instilled in her an appreciation for building things and a confidence that anything can be fixed if you are willing to work on it for a while.

Meeting Kristina's Dad

I'll never forget my first encounter with Mr. Kenner. Kristina and I had been dating for several months and we were getting serious about our relationship. A couple of days after her dad returned from Puerto Rico, I went to her house to meet him, before we went out on our date. I drove my truck over to their condo, knocked on the front door, and was greeted by a frowning 6'4" man who stooped over to look me in the eye.

"Hello, Mr. Kenner, I'm Mark Buckley, Kristina's friend. Welcome back to California."

He tilted his head to the side, motioning me to come in. As I tried to step through the door he was partially blocking, he leered into my face and spoke with an alcohol-drenched voice, "The last time I met a guy like you, I threw a brick in his face!"

I took two more steps into the condo's living room. I didn't know what to do or what to say. I felt like fleeing through the front door and never seeing him again. Just then Kristina came into the room and gave me a quick hug. She was the real reason I was there. I loved her and knew from the stories she had told me that her dad had a drinking problem. I also knew she loved him very much.

I decided to stick it out, for better or for worse, because Kristina was worth more to me than whatever hassles or danger her dad posed. Even as a self-centered kid, I got along well with my friends' parents. Now as a follower of Christ, I believed in the teaching of Ephesians 6:2–3, "Honor your father and mother, so you can have a good life and a long life."

I just wished her dad wasn't so big. A big, cantankerous guy can be intimidating.

Before Kristina and I left for the evening, I made small talk with Mr. Kenner for a few minutes. Years later, I realized the greeting he gave me that night was probably his way of determining if I was out to harm his daughter.

If I had simply wanted to sleep with Kristina, I would have left that night and never returned. I had better intentions. We kissed a lot, but we didn't have a sexual relationship until we got married two years later. And because of my love for Kristina, I built a relationship with Charles Kenner, who, in time, became a blessing to me.

In those days, Trident Builders took every job offered to us. We continued to be the lowest bidders for most jobs, because we had almost no overhead and we only billed our labor costs at four dollars an hour. There weren't even immigrants competing for work with us in Marin in the early 1970s. However, it took us longer to finish jobs than it would have taken experienced men.

One day, we got a job installing a linoleum tile floor in a large kitchen in Terra Linda. I had never done floor work before. Mr. Kenner came to the job the first morning and showed me how to start from the center of the floor and work my way toward each wall. Working out from the center is critical to keeping the tiles perfectly squared, as well as finishing evenly at the walls.

On another job site, Mr. Kenner showed up and saw I was using two or three men to lay every brick along a pathway bordered by a small wall. We had one man holding the brick while the others tried to keep the mortar from falling off the sides of the brick while it was being fitted into place. I knew we were being inefficient, but I didn't know any alternative.

Mr. Kenner cursed at our naïve approach. He pulled out a trowel and slapped some mortar on a brick. With another quick swipe of the trowel along the opposite side of the mortar, he created suction that held the mortar in place. He showed us how you can hold a brick with the mortar facing down and it won't fall off because of the suction created by the proper double swipe of the trowel. Every experienced bricklayer understands this simple procedure that saves time, hassle, and mess.

Thoughts of Marriage

As we continued to date, I thought about marrying Kristina, but the idea of marriage scared me. I watched Bob and Carol Gaulden at Solid Rock and admired the love and kindness they showed each other. However, my parents were divorced, and I didn't know any couples my age that had good marriages.

At the same time, I struggled with remaining celibate and would have probably given in to sex; fortunately, Kristina resisted my advances when they were inappropriate.

Kristina's parents had separated because of her dad's alcoholism. Kristina then moved into the home of Kent and Bobbie Philpott. To support herself, she painted houses with Kent and a small crew. She also attended College of Marin, where she was preparing to go into the nursing program. In addition, she babysat the Philpotts' three children several times a week.

I led Trident Builders during the day. We had Bible studies, prayer meetings, or evangelism most evenings, so both of us were busy day and night. Often, we were only able to spend one evening a week together. I was frustrated by our lack of time together. When we did go out, we would often argue about little things.

Kristina and I loved to kiss and hug, but we were careful to keep our relationship celibate. On the occasions when I started moving my hands to caress her with too much intimacy, she would push my hands away. I could sense she wanted a sexual relationship as much as I did, but she loved Jesus too much to allow us to become sexual before marriage. I respected her even more for her discipline and faithfulness to God.

Yet, I still wasn't ready to take the next step. Marriage scared me.

Shelly

My relationship with Kristina had stalled. She was beautiful and intelligent. She loved the Lord, and she loved me. I thought I loved her, but I wasn't ready to ask her to marry me. I had lost the sense of excitement we had when we first dated. Perhaps my parents' divorce had scarred me. I believed marriage was for life, and I didn't want any doubts when I took that step.

One night our relationship was almost permanently derailed.

I took Kristina to a fondue restaurant in Corte Madera, where all the customers sat at long tables together. Our waiter brought us a big fondue pot of melted cheese heated by a flame. As we were dipping our bread cubes into the cheese, the door opened and a group from Jews for Jesus walked into the restaurant. I waved to a couple I recognized, and the entire group came over to sit with us. I was stunned to realize that one of the girls was the cover girl for the *Christian LIFE Magazine* I helped distribute in Dallas. She sat down at the table right across from us.

I introduced myself and learned her name was Shelly. As Kristina visited with some of the other Jews for Jesus, Shelly and I stared into each other's eyes across the table. I was totally smitten with her and asked her for her phone number before the evening was over.

I decided to break up with Kristina the next week. The next day I called Shelly and soon started dating her. I felt guilty about what I did, but I felt it would be a mistake for me to marry Kristina as long as I wondered if there was someone better for me. I had a couple of memorable dates with Shelly that helped me understand whom I should marry.

One day, Shelly and I drove to the University of the Pacific in Stockton, where I was speaking about the Lord to a contemporary affairs class. On the way, I picked up a strange-looking hitchhiker. The guy was wearing long dark pants, several shirts, two coats, and two baseball caps. One of the caps was pointed straight, the other angled up 45 degrees. He also had a piece of transparent tape across his lower lip. He joined us in the front seat of my truck. Shelly looked at me like I was trying to get her killed. She scooted over as close to me as possible to avoid touching him.

He seemed like a homeless wanderer, and I wanted to talk with him about Jesus as we drove. I tried to be friendly, but he wasn't very responsive. Finally, my curiosity got the best of me. I asked the man if he realized he had a piece of tape across his lip.

He looked at me like I was stupid. He told me he had it there on purpose. He explained the tape helped keep the sun off his lip. I guess the tape was a lot cheaper than Chapstick and probably as effective; however, I don't think it will ever catch on with the public.

We dropped the guy off and continued driving to the university. Shelly was angry with me for picking him up.

My next date with her was our last one. We had been attending Grace Church, where Shelly's brother-in-law, Paul Bryant, was the pastor. On Sunday, after the church service, I decided to take her to a romantic beach at the end of Bear Valley Trail in the Point Reyes National Seashore. We needed to be back by six o'clock because I was teaching a Sunday school class an hour before the seven o'clock evening service. This turned out to be more of a problem than I had anticipated.

I loaded two bikes in the back of my truck. We stopped and bought sandwiches for a picnic, then drove twenty-five miles to the trailhead. From the trailhead, there was an eight-mile trail to the beach. It had several ups and downs as it wound through the tall coastal trees. Shelly didn't ride bikes often, so we took our time, stopping at a couple of meadows along the way. We eventually got to the beach. We sat in the sand and enjoyed a picnic lunch, talked, and watched sea otters playing in the surf.

I saw a man walking along the quiet beach, and it suddenly occurred to me that it was getting late. I asked the man if he knew what time it was, and he told me it was 4:45. Doing a quick calculation, I realized it would take Shelly more than an hour to ride the trail back to the parking lot. It was a forty-minute drive from there to the church, which meant I was going to be late to teach the Sunday school class.

I knew I could get there a lot faster if I left Shelly and hurried back alone. I told her the problem and suggested that she enjoy the beach and ride back to the trailhead at a leisurely pace. I would hurry back to the truck, drive to the church, teach the class, and then drive back to pick her up as soon as I could. She reluctantly agreed with my plan.

I pedaled as fast as I could back up the trail and drove rapidly to the church. I arrived just in time to teach the class. Afterward, as I started to leave, I saw Pastor Paul. He asked me where Shelly was. He became upset when I told him she was on her way by bike to the Bear Valley Trailhead. When I got back to the trailhead, it was 8 P.M., pitch dark, and cold. Shelly was the only one in the parking lot. She didn't have a coat or sweater. She was shivering and not happy at all.

These experiences helped me realize that Kristina was the right woman for me. Shelly and I broke up. She eventually married a friend of mine named Bruce, and they had four children.

While Kristina had never been a cover girl, she was and is beautiful. Most importantly, I knew she had the right heart, mind, and spirit for me. I had deeply hurt Kristina, but fortunately, she was willing to take me back. There is no such thing as a perfect match between imperfect people. Every couple must work out the challenges that come when two people living in this sinful world get married. However, having peace about the person you decide to marry is critical.

Engaged

In the spring of 1973, I moved out of my mom's house and took over the leadership of Solid Rock. I had done all I could to help my mom the preceding eighteen months. Now, at twenty-three, I felt ready to start a new phase in my life.

My relationship with Kristina had gotten more serious. And I was looking for wisdom as I wrestled with whether to ask her to marry me.

When I told my dad I was in love with Kristina, he replied, "I don't want to know if you love her; I want to know if you like her." My dad's advice was practical. He knew that good marriages depend on mutual respect and the ability to enjoy life together. Feelings of romance can ebb and flow. If couples like being together and sharing the simple tasks of life, they have a better chance of a successful marriage.

My dad didn't understand the value of a covenant in marriage. I felt the weight of marriage, because I fully intended to stay sexually faithful to my wife all the days of my life.

I really did like Kristina. I liked talking and praying with her. I liked taking her to my job sites. She was not only interested in our construction projects; she often had practical advice and suggestions. I respected her intelligence, her work ethic, and her love for Jesus. We would often argue because we were both strong-willed and opinionated, but we had fun together.

Searching for wisdom, I went to Corte Madera to talk with Father Todd Ewald, a spirit-filled Episcopalian priest. I asked him how I would know when it was God's timing for me to get married. He replied, "When you have the peace that passes understanding, you will know the time is right."

As Father Ewald said those words, I felt the peace of the Lord come over me. I still wasn't ready to propose to Kristina, but the Lord had shown me through the Spirit that I would have this peace when the time was right.

A few weeks later, I decided to stay home alone at Solid Rock on a Sunday afternoon after church. I had been invited to a party, but for some reason I just didn't have the energy to go. As I was lying on the couch, I heard a knock on the door and was surprised to see Kristina. I invited her in, and we sat on the couch and began to talk.

After a few minutes, I paused, looked into her beautiful hazel eyes and asked, "Will you marry me?"

She paused for a minute and then smiled. "Yes!"

Before we even had a chance to kiss, the front door opened, and David Summers, one of the men who lived at Solid Rock, walked into the living room.

"David, I asked Kristina to marry me," I announced to him.

"That's what I hear," he replied.

"You couldn't have heard it already. I just made the decision and asked her today, and I wasn't even planning it!"

David walked away with a smirk. Maybe it was inevitable to him, but it was news to me.

Kristina's Dad, Charles Kenner

Three days later, I took Kristina's dad to lunch. I knew how much Kristina loved her dad and I wanted to honor him. During lunch, I asked Mr. Kenner for his permission to marry Kristina. We both felt mature, but she was just nineteen years old. Mr. Kenner gave me his blessing with one caveat: "Good women are hard to handle, and Kristina is one g—d— good woman." I wished he hadn't used the Lord's name in vain, but I got his point.

When we met for lunch, Charles Kenner was struggling in a

major way. Kristina's mom had left him several months earlier. He was living in an old run-down hotel in San Rafael. He had been drinking a lot and was depressed about being alone. Before Christmas, he had come to the Church of the Open Door with us. Bob Hymers preached a sermon on Hell that night. At the end of his message, he invited people to accept the Lord. Mr. Kenner raised his hand to accept Christ. This gave us comfort, but Charles was still a troubled soul.

A few weeks after our lunch, he got drunk one afternoon and called Kristina. He told her he had taken an overdose of pills. She called 911 and the paramedics were able to get him to the hospital and save his life. Kristina became distressed. She worried that her dad would eventually kill himself.

On March 19, 1973, Charles called Kristina after overdosing again. Kristina called the police to go and check on him. He was able to answer the door and assured the officer that he was fine. The next day, Kristina's younger brother, Kirk, stopped by the hotel to see how their dad was doing. Kirk found Charles Kenner dead in his little room.

Over the years, I occasionally find Kristina crying. I have learned not to take it personally. She often still cries because she misses her dad.

Our Wedding

Kristina and I set our wedding date for August 12, 1973. Since we were paying for everything ourselves, there were no restrictions on who we invited. We decided to invite everyone we knew and loved to join us on our special day. We had hundreds of the invitations we designed printed. Inside my truck, I put a stack of invitations, which I gave to friends I ran into and a few hitchhikers I picked up before our wedding day.

The week before our wedding, Kristina and I went on a picnic that proved to be pivotal for our relationship. Before eating lunch, we spread out a blanket under a tree on a grassy hillside. As we began to talk, we were both excited about our upcoming marriage. But after a while, I could sense something was troubling Kristina. I'm not always perceptive or real compassionate, but I wanted to help with whatever was bothering her.

I asked her a few questions, and she told me a heartbreaking story.

Kristina's mother, Betty, was an alcoholic. She had tried to commit suicide four times when Kristina was young. On one occasion, Betty shot herself with a 45-caliber pistol. She pointed the gun at her heart and fired. The gun kicked upward as she pulled the trigger, and the bullet went through her shoulder. A few years later, she slit her wrists to the bone and was hospitalized for four months in the mental ward of Mendocino State Hospital. During that time, Kristina's dad brought in a housekeeper with a fourteen-year-old son to help care for Kristina and her younger brother, Kirk. At the time, Kristina was nine years old and Kirk was seven years old. Through tears, Kristina told me that the housekeeper's son had molested her.

I was stunned. Kristina was carrying a lot of pain in her soul. I didn't understand the implications being molested can have in a woman's life, but I could see she was really hurting. I believed Jesus Christ has the power to heal our bodies and our souls.

1 John 3:8 says the Son of Man came to destroy the work of the evil one.

Kristina had a big wound and a big need. We serve a big God, and I knew we needed to ask Him to heal and deliver her right then and there.

I put my hands on her shoulders. We began to pray, and I commanded every demonic force that had tormented her to leave her. We asked Jesus to heal the pain in her heart. As we prayed, her body began to shake. She sobbed deeply as the Holy Spirit touched her. Under that tree's shade, Jesus healed Kristina's soul and delivered her from the evil one.

By the time we finished praying, I felt that Kristina was going to be fine. God healed her in a way that made her healthier than ever. If I had not heard her describe her past and had not seen the Lord touch her myself, I would never have known of her awful experiences. In our long life together, I've never seen any negative effect from the abuse she suffered. The Lord's healing made her pain redemptive. She has since shared her testimony and helped many other women experience healing.

The following week, we bought hams, turkeys, roasts, and drinks from Scotty's Market for our wedding reception. Scotty's meat department cooked, sliced, and placed the meat on trays for the cost of the meat, plus one dollar per item. We bought a wedding cake, and ordered rolls and salads from a local deli. On a beautiful sunny Sunday afternoon, more than 400 hungry people showed up for our wedding.

Trinity Assembly of God Church in San Rafael had not finished its remodeling project the day we got married. This meant

Kristina and her bridesmaids literally walked the plank in the form of two 12-inch-wide boards that spanned the walkway into the church. I entered with Kent and the groomsmen and saw the sanctuary packed with people. They came from our ministry, our work, our families, as well as our friends. I was so nervous that the ceremony was mostly a blur for me. Afterward, our friends served a great lunch under the trees as singers serenaded the guests.

While everyone else was eating, Kristina and I stood in a reception line for more than an hour greeting guests. Moishe Rosen, the founder of Jews for Jesus, prayed a special blessing over us when he came through the line. We have followed his example and prayed God's blessings on many other couples when we have attended their weddings ever since.

Mickey Parsen also came through the reception line. He gave us our biggest and most surprising wedding gift—his 1972 Ford truck with a camper shell, which was in perfect condition. He had loaned the truck to our ministry for several weeks prior to the wedding. I had been using it to take my construction crew to jobs and kids to our Bible studies. We really needed the truck, and with less than $1,000 to our name after our wedding, the truck was the perfect gift for us.

Kristina and I rode off from our wedding celebration on a tandem bicycle that was a gift from my brothers. It was a great getaway vehicle. We rode it to our new pickup truck, which was hidden a few blocks away to keep it from being decorated by our zealous young friends.

After changing clothes at my mom's house, we headed north toward Lake Tahoe for our honeymoon. Our destination was a house owned by Bob and Diane Ellison that was on a hill overlooking Meek's Bay.

Our Honeymoon

We drove toward Tahoe for an hour, stopped in Fairfield, and spent our first night together at the Holiday Inn. We were both nervous when we got into the room and closed the door. We got down on our knees and dedicated our marriage to the Lord. As we prayed, the Spirit of God took our insecurities away. The Lord brought a blessing to our relationship that has remained until this day.

The next day I stopped to pick up a hitchhiker as we pulled out of a gas station near the Holiday Inn. Kristina and I were so happy to be together, we radiated the joy of the Lord. The hitchhiker marveled at our new truck, which we explained was a gift from God. He could sense our joy, and he prayed with us to accept the Lord before we dropped him off an hour later.

When we arrived at the Ellison's house at Lake Tahoe, I searched for a shaded spot in the forest where I could spend time alone with the Lord. I found a spot under the pine trees not far from the house, and I walked there with my Bible. I spread a towel over the soft pine needles in the shade to create a comfortable spot for prayer and study. I visited this spot each day.

It would be inappropriate for me to describe all the blessings we experienced over the next several days. Those days confirmed to me that it is well worth the wait for those who obey the Lord and stay celibate before marriage. Even though Kristina and I had both been sexually active before we started following Christ, our sins had been forgiven and our souls had been healed. We started our marriage with clear consciences and a sense of God's blessing. This has been a source of strength for us ever since.

One afternoon, as I was praying in the pine forest, I had a vision of Jesus placing His hands on my head as I knelt before Him. He blessed me and anointed me. He didn't speak to me directly, but an idea came to me at that moment. The idea was to call men to meet in small groups to connect with the Lord through prayer and sharing their lives with one another.

I hoped to see that vision fulfilled, and over the years it came to pass in wonderful ways. I've started several groups with men who meet weekly to pray and share their lives together. These have been a great source of wisdom and encouragement for me for many years.

The Ellisons' home at Lake Tahoe was a three-story house. For the second week of our honeymoon we invited the six men who were going to live with us at Solid Rock to join us. We were going to be one spiritual family, so I thought we should share the week together. It is one of several things I would skip if I were living my life over again.

The following weekend, I left Kristina with the guys at Tahoe and drove to the Methodist church in Terra Linda. It would be my first time preaching in a church on Sunday morning. As I left, the men were helping Kristina paint the exterior of the house. It was our way of thanking the Ellisons for allowing us to use it for two weeks.

Lacking Wisdom

When I arrived at the Methodist church in Terra Linda, I was shocked to see Susan Anderson, a girl I had known since grammar school. She was the church organist. In the fourth grade, a group of us had picked on Susan. We made fun of her freckles and her reading skills. I had freckles too, but nobody was taunting me about them or my mistakes reading out loud. We were being cruel to a young girl who couldn't defend herself. A wise woman taught us a great lesson about our behavior.

Bill Hitchcock's mom found out Bill, Jeff, and I were making fun of Susan. She made us an offer we couldn't refuse. If we would be nice to Susan for one month, she would allow us to have a party. Mrs. Hitchcock suggested we invite the girls we liked from our class to the Hitchcocks' house for a dance.

We accepted her offer and stopped teasing Susan. A month later, we had the first dance party any of us had ever attended. However, when the party started that night, there was a problem. None of us knew how to talk to the girls we had invited. We had stared at them and teased them in class, but once we were at the party, the girls were all on one side of the Hitchcocks' family room, and the boys were on the other side.

Finally, Mrs. Hitchcock put on a dance record called "Delilah Jones." I'll always remember that song because it was the only record we had that night. The flip side of the 45-rpm was a song nobody liked, and Mrs. Hitchcock didn't have any other records.

By the second or third time she played "Delilah Jones," one of the guys got the courage to walk across the room to ask a girl to dance. Then, one by one, the rest of us followed. I started dancing with Cynthia, a beautiful brunette who I had a crush on that year. Even though we were old enough to know it was strange to dance all night to the same three-minute song, the party was a huge success. We had a great time, and several of us fell in love that night.

The next week in school, we were too shy to approach the girls we were in love with. However, we never bothered Susan Anderson again. After the party, we started being friendly toward Susan and felt bad we had been mean to her.

Mrs. Hitchcock died when she was still a young mother. But before she died, she had taught a group of self-centered young bullies there is a better way to live. I'll always be thankful for her love and her wisdom.

When I walked into the church and saw Susan, I spoke to her for the first time since grammar school. I asked her forgiveness for being such a jerk toward her when we were young. She accepted my apology, and I was able to preach effectively to their church that morning.

With more wisdom, I would have never left my new wife with the guys at Solid Rock to go preach when we were still on our honeymoon. Nor would I have moved into Solid Rock and had my new wife live with six other men in the first place. I would also have waited a couple more years before moving into the leadership of the discipleship house.

We don't get do-overs in life based on hindsight, but we can get a few redemptive stories.

I made these decisions so I could be available to do ministry. I did get the ministry experience I wanted, and thankfully, Kristina persevered and prospered through it all.

Looking back, I can see that through the grace of God, I married a woman who loved me and rarely complained even though she didn't get a lot of attention. I was immersed in ministry and assumed my lifestyle was normal for someone who loved Jesus.

CHAPTER TWENTY

SOLID ROCK
DISCIPLESHIP HOUSE

After our honeymoon, Kristina and I returned to Solid Rock on Wilson Avenue in Novato. The next few months gave us great learning experiences.

Along with the six men who lived with us, we had regular visitors. Occasionally, the police would stop by and drop off somebody who needed a place to live. We would also get calls from mental health officials when their facility at Marin General Hospital was full. If they needed a place to put someone with mental issues, they sent the person to us. We made room for some strange characters.

It got to the point that our neighbors wanted us to keep our doors locked. They didn't worry someone might break into our house; neither did we. The bad guys were already inside. They worried some of these guys would get out of our house and come into theirs.

Dinner Disaster

We still tell the story about the first time Kristina and I invited another couple over to have dinner at Solid Rock. Our guests were Art and Joanne Sorenson, who were old enough to be our parents.

204 FROM DARKNESS INTO LIGHT

Art was the pastor of All Saints Lutheran Church in Novato. I wanted to get to know him better and let him see what we were doing in our ministry.

The Sorensons came over for dinner about 5:30 P.M., and we sat in the living room and talked. Kristina had put chicken, squash, and potatoes in the oven to cook while we all enjoyed the fellowship. All the men in the house were home, and they joined our conversation and shared some of their testimonies with Art and Joanne.

By 6:30, we were all hungry. Kristina went into the kitchen to take our dinner out of the oven. She quickly returned and asked to talk with me. When I walked into the kitchen, she opened the oven, and I could see that the food was still raw. The oven was broken and had never started. I told her to work on the dinner, and I would take care of our guests.

There was only one working burner on the stove, but Kristina turned it on and got the chicken started. I told the Sorensons we were going to have a delayed dinner because the oven was broken. I suggested that we have a time of prayer together. We all started to pray, although Art didn't seem too enthusiastic, and Joanne stayed quiet.

I then suggested we take communion. It didn't occur to me at the time they would have probably preferred a glass of wine and some hors d'oeuvres rather than a sip of grape juice with a bit of broken matzo. We didn't drink alcohol at Solid Rock and we hadn't planned on hors d'oeuvres, but I was good at conversation. Meanwhile, Kristina was frantically trying to cook a three-course dinner on a one-burner stove. There were no microwaves in those days.

Finally, around 7:30, just as Kristina was finishing the dinner, Art stood up and said that they would have to get going because they had another meeting that night. I tried to stall them, but he was adamant. We ended up putting some chicken in a brown paper bag, and they took it to go. As the rest of us sat down to eat, I realized it was going to be harder than I anticipated to impress the local pastors about the legitimacy of our ministry.

As time passed, other problems arose, which also provided good stories years later.

Some of the guys who lived with us ended up becoming pastors and leaders. Others left our house and ended up in jail. We loved them all. And over time, we learned to love them with more wisdom.

Doing Too Much

One day, Peter Battaglia, a young man who lived with us for a couple of years, seemed distraught. I asked him what was wrong. He looked at me and explained, "Mark, you wake me up in the morning and tell me it's time to go to work. Then you say the blessing over our breakfast. Then we go to work all day, and you are the boss. Then we come home, and you say the blessing at our dinner. Then we go to a Bible study and you teach us the Bible. I don't know if I can take it anymore!"

Peter had a point. I don't know if I could have taken it either. My motives were good. I provided jobs for the guys on our construction crew. We were no longer holding our money in common at Solid Rock. We all worked and chipped in $300 a month toward rent and food. We were learning carpentry, masonry, and construction skills as we went from job to job.

Nevertheless, I was not Peter's dad, and I couldn't be his savior either. Sometimes, the only way we learn when "enough is enough" is when we do too much. I discovered the hard way that doing for others what they should be doing for themselves does not bear good fruit.

Malcolm confirmed this insight. He was usually the last to climb into my truck on the way to work each day. He spent more time in the bathroom combing his hair than most guys do. His habit of making us wait was frustrating, but I got used to it.

The day came when Malcolm was going to move back to New York to be with his family. I drove him to San Francisco, so he could take a Greyhound bus. Malcolm bought his ticket and I waited in line with him, so I could say good-bye when he boarded the bus.

A few minutes before boarding time, Malcolm decided to go to the bathroom. I told him to hurry. Soon after he left, the bus driver appeared and began taking tickets as the passengers boarded. Malcolm was nowhere to be seen. As the last passenger boarded, I told the bus driver that Malcolm had a ticket and should be appearing any minute. The driver said he would wait, but he wouldn't wait long.

I ran back to the restroom, where I found Malcolm combing his hair. I practically dragged him out to the bus, but by the time we got there it was too late. The bus had departed for New York without him. Malcolm was able to take another bus to Sacramento, where he caught up with the bus to New York, but it was a big hassle.

I realized as I drove home, all the waiting I did for Malcolm taught him the wrong lesson. The rest of the world was not going to wait patiently for him.

Supporting those who are not being responsible is teaching them the wrong lesson. Doing for others what they should be doing for themselves is codependency, not love. Misguided love does not prepare anyone for a fruitful future.

The truths Kristina and I learned leading Solid Rock would eventually help us in the years to come, not only with our own children, but also with countless others who would join our ministries over the years.

Overwhelmed

We were on the go seven days a week. Our Bible studies in Novato were growing and so were our ministries.

One night, I had a dream that startled me. I was inside a theater when a neutron explosion went off. The explosion released a powerful wave of energy, but it didn't destroy matter. I grabbed a pillar that was holding up the theater's balcony. My body flapped like a flag in a storm as waves of energy pulsated through me. In a few minutes the energy wave passed, and my body collapsed beside the pillar.

I woke up exhausted and drenched with sweat. Emotionally, I felt as if the dream had been real. I immediately had an interpretation. The intensity of our ministry and work responsibilities was overwhelming me. I hoped the dream signified that the wave of intensity had passed, and we were going to enter a season that would be more balanced.

In hindsight, we were still in the middle of that intensity. Some of it was circumstantial, but much of it was self-induced stress.

One of the manifestations that Kristina and I were not living a well-balanced lifestyle came early in our marriage, with heartbreaking news.

Miscarriage

Kristina became pregnant about four months after our wedding. We were both excited about having a baby. A few days after getting the news, we told her mother, my mother, and many of our friends. Kristina had a wonderful glow about her in the early weeks of her pregnancy. But our pace of life remained intense.

One day she started experiencing severe cramps followed by bleeding. The next day, she had a miscarriage. The excitement of her pregnancy had turned to grief. The little baby we were looking forward to meeting was dead. We prayed together and named the baby *Isaac*.

Our miscarriage stunned me. I had been confident we were living the life God wanted us to live. I was aware there were promises in the Old Testament that God would bless His people and they would not have miscarriages. I couldn't understand why this pain had come into our lives.

As I prayed, the only thing I could imagine being out of order in our lives was the intensity of our pace. We were living with six other men at Solid Rock. Kristina was shopping, cooking, cleaning, and doing laundry for all of us. We were not keeping the Sabbath, but I thought the Sabbath no longer mattered because we were following Jesus.

I had a philosophy in those days that we are all given a certain amount of energy to use each day. When we go to sleep, we got replenished and received a new portion of energy for the next day.

I also believed that if we went to sleep at night without using all the energy God gave us, we had wasted the energy. This meant we had not served the Lord with our whole mind, heart, soul, and strength. This philosophy motivated me to keep an intense pace for many years. It took twenty years before I understood how dangerous my philosophy was. Eventually, seven days a week of intense ministry year after year left me so depleted that I had to be hospitalized. I learned you can have a good motivation and still get bad results.

From this experience, I finally realized the Lord commands us to take a Sabbath day for many good reasons. For one, we don't really recover all our energy every night. No matter how well we sleep when we are young, we need rest days to help restore our bodies and souls. We gradually dissipate our physical and emotional reserves each week. Hebrews 3 and 4 teach that God desires us to enter His rest as a part of our physical and spiritual lifestyle.

People in ministry never have all their work finished. Sabbath days are meant to teach us to trust the Lord, so we can live a lifestyle of faith and rest. It takes faith to rest when there is always more work to be done. Tithing can teach us to trust the Lord with our finances. Most people who tithe could really use the ten percent they give to the Lord for other purposes. However, those who tithe experience God's provision in ways that helps them realize God is providing for them all the time. Keeping a Sabbath is one-seventh of your time. It is a great challenge in a busy world, but the Sabbath can provide great benefits.

When we trust God and rest, He can give us insights and understanding, which make us more fruitful in the long run than we would be if we worked seven days a week.

The bottom line is that the Lord has made the Sabbath for man because we need it. I am not advocating for spiritual legalism. I am encouraging you to set aside time to rest so you can be healthy. God rewards our obedience, and eventually the truths of Scripture are revealed to those who obey them.

CHAPTER TWENTY-ONE

LIFESTYLE CHANGES

Problems at Solid Rock

I did not have a clue about the real nature of women before Kristina and I were married. I naïvely assumed living in a discipleship house with six men would at least give Kristina and me something to talk about. It did give us something to talk about, but not in the way I imagined, nor in the way she had hoped when she married me.

There was always some sort of mess with the men at Solid Rock.

Kristina did house painting with Kent and several others, so she had professional quality paintbrushes in our garage. Several times, one of the guys would take her brushes and paint something with lead-based paint. They would often fail to clean the brushes. Kristina was not happy when her paintbrushes were carelessly ruined.

One by one, our wedding presents were also destroyed. We received eight sets of eight drinking glasses from guests at our wedding. I thought we had enough glasses to last a lifetime. However, I underestimated how many glasses men in a hurry could break when washing dishes by hand. We would sometimes have two glasses broken in the same night. Within two years, almost all our glasses had been broken.

One night, Kristina came home and found one of the brothers was cleaning the carburetor of his car on our kitchen stove. He was soaking his carburetor in muriatic acid in the pressure cooker we had been given for a wedding present. We were fortunate he did not cause an explosion when he heated up the acid. The acid totally corroded the inside of the pressure cooker, which had been one of Kristina's favorite presents.

One day, while talking on the phone with my dad, he said something that changed our lives. I told him how proud I was of Kristina, and I began filling him in on all the things she was doing to take care of our domestic chores. After listening for a few minutes, my dad shouted at me over the phone. "If you don't stop having your wife do the laundry for those bums who live with you, I'm going to come up there and throw them all out of that house!"

I knew he meant what he said. I also believed I should honor my father. My dad gave me very few directives after I became a teenager. So, on the rare times he was adamant about something, I took it to heart. After I hung up the phone, I went to find Kristina and fill her in on our conversation.

She was happy to hear she was going to be free from doing the laundry for the other guys. They missed the benefit, but there were no complaints.

As I reflected on my dad's counsel, I realized I had been asking Kristina to do more than was healthy for her. I didn't ever want to make that mistake again.

Moving

When the ongoing pressure got to the point that neither of us wanted to go home after a long day at work, we knew something had to change.

About that time, Frank Novak, our landlord on Wilson Avenue, decided he wanted to sell the house. We quickly found a nicer, smaller, four-bedroom house on Trumbull Road and moved Solid Rock. Our rent increased from $285 to $400 a month, and we went from six men living with us to two men and two women. Nancy and Sandy had recently joined our ministry. They were more helpful around the house than the men were.

Kristina began raising rabbits in our backyard for food. One day, she told me that rats had snatched a couple of her baby rabbits out of their cages. She wanted to get a cat to deal with the rats. I resisted her idea. Our house was crowded with people and I didn't want a cat. She believed wives should submit to their husbands, but she had ways of exerting influence. Within a week, we owned a cat.

One afternoon while Sandy was home alone at Solid Rock, she heard a scratching sound at the front door. She opened the door and saw our cat with a big rat dangling from his mouth. Sandy screamed. The cat dropped the rat, and the rat ran into our house! It found an opening in the cabinet wall underneath our kitchen sink and disappeared into it.

It was a funny story when Sandy told it to us, but we wondered what became of the rat. It didn't take long to find out. Within a few days, a foul smell developed in the kitchen. It got progressively worse. We realized the rat had died and was decomposing inside the wall behind the sink.

Kristina bought deodorizers, but the stench overwhelmed them. The decomposing rodent began to smell so bad that we left

214 FROM DARKNESS INTO LIGHT

our front door and windows open in a vain attempt to clear the air. Our rented house had no screens on the doors or windows. Our neighbors on Trumbull Road kept horses on their property. The rat smell attracted horse flies from their pasture. The flies swirled, dived, and invaded our house.

We hosted Bible studies twice a week and had a lot of visitors in our home. For the first two weeks, when visitors came over, we explained the situation and apologized for the stink. As the weeks went on, we almost got used to the foul smell in our house. When we forgot to explain the problem, guests would give us strange looks. They smelled something foul and saw horse flies swirling inside our house. They undoubtedly wondered what kind of weird, redneck Christians we were.

Expanding

At the Christian General Store, we held several evening prayer meetings in 1973 that had a major impact on our movement. Many of our leaders had spent the day fasting and praying before our prayer meeting. We hoped to get a clear sense of what God wanted us to do next. That night during the prayer time, we felt like the Holy Spirit directed us to start a ministry in San Francisco. We hoped to start a Christian General Store, Bible studies, and discipleship houses, just as we had in San Rafael. Don Micheletti volunteered to lead the new ministry.

A few days after the prayer meeting, Don and I drove to San Francisco and located a building on Taravel Street that was perfect for the ministry he would start. We had received a gift of $20,000, which we used to rent the building, build shelves, and stock the store with merchandise. We opened a Christian General Store, and Don started teaching Bible studies in the back room each week. Don had a work ethic like few men I have ever met. He completed his bachelor's degree at the University of San Francisco while he was leading the ministry and working evenings at the juvenile hall. After his graduation, he and his wife, Bonnie, eventually moved to Sonoma. In Sonoma, while building a house for his family, Don earned his master's degree. At the same time, he launched The Church of the Open Door, The Christian General Store, and the Open Door Christian School in Sonoma.

Don eventually took his family to Oral Roberts University in Oklahoma, where he began medical school. He ultimately graduated from Johns Hopkins in Baltimore and became an MD.

Joining Forces

Our Lucas Valley Sunday night service had been going for six months when Kent and I decided to hold a prayer meeting for pastors. We invited several pastors to join us one Friday night at the Christian General Store in San Rafael. We were hoping to pray for and encourage one another in our ministries.

The only other pastor who showed up for the meeting was Bob Hymers. Kent and I prayed for Bob, and then we started sharing ministry ideas with each other. Bob suggested that we merge House Ministries with the Church of the Open Door. House Ministries consisted of a couple hundred young people who attended our Bible studies, as well as those who lived in our discipleship houses. We also owned the Christian General Stores. Our ministries stretched from San Francisco to Petaluma.

Kent and I had resisted the idea of starting Sunday morning services, but as we listened to Bob's offer, we began to reconsider our position. Many people who were in the Church of the Open Door had originally been in House Ministries. A merger would simply acknowledge the reality that we had common roots and a common desire to make more disciples for Christ. We told Bob we liked the idea and would give him a final answer after we spoke with the rest of our leaders.

In November 1973, we merged House Ministries with the Church of the Open Door. The pastoral team consisted of Bob Hymers, Mike Riley, and Roger Hoffman from the Open Door, along with Kent, Ken Sanders, and me from House Ministries.

We also asked Dick Bruener to join us. Dick became the chairman of our board of elders. Kent and Bob had met Dick at Golden Gate Seminary and believed he could be a neutral, mature leader we could all respect. Dick had come to Golden Gate Seminary from a Jesus People ministry in Houston. I had not known Dick, but he was respected by the men who were acquainted with him. Kent and Bob were both strong personalities, and we assumed Dick would prevent either of them from dominating the new church.

We announced the merger, and about one hundred people joined us for the first Sunday service of the Church of the Open Door at Scout Hall in Mill Valley. Within a few weeks, we moved to the Carpenter's Hall in San Rafael.

We established a preaching rotation that featured Kent and Bob, but also occasionally included Ken Sanders, Roger Hoffman, Dick Bruener, and me. We kept that rotation for the next two years. Every Sunday, we would sing a couple of hymns and several praise songs. We had people give testimonies and share how Christ delivered them from sin. The sermons lasted 45 minutes and were followed by an altar call for people to commit their lives to Christ. Every Sunday, no matter who was preaching, people responded to the call to make Jesus the Lord and Savior of their lives.

Our services were edifying and fruitful. With people getting saved each week, the church grew. We added a second service on Sunday mornings and formed discipleship houses for many of the new converts. Our pastors wore sport coats and ties on Sundays. Ken and I were paid $300 a month, Kent and Dick received $400, and Bob was given $600 because he did not have any other income. The rest of us supplemented our incomes by leading discipleship houses and working in construction or house painting.

Our church was thriving on Sundays, but our Monday morning pastors' meetings were tumultuous. Kent and Bob had strong disagreements about how a church should be run. Dick, our moderator, was not able to restrain them. We were like a young, immature family that loves one another but argues a lot. We didn't know how to relate any other way. Kent and Bob might be yelling at each other at 10:00 A.M., but by the afternoon they would be laughing and talking like nothing had happened.

The leadership meetings were exhausting and troubling to me, but it was obvious God was blessing our ministries despite our dysfunctional behavior. It wasn't until years later that I learned how to lead elders in a positive and constructive way.

Deliverance Ministry

As our church in San Rafael grew, our ministries in San

Francisco, Novato, and Petaluma grew as well. In each of those cities we established discipleship houses, Bible studies, and a Christian General Store.

We held evangelism outreaches on the streets every Friday night, and often went into San Francisco and handed out gospel tracts in North Beach. When people responded to Christ, we would take them to whichever discipleship house had room for them.

Many of the people we brought off the streets to our houses had been involved in drugs and the occult. Those in the worst condition were often taken to Berachah House in Petaluma. [*Berachah* is the Hebrew word for "blessing".] Berachah House, run by Ken and Mary Sanders, was our discipleship house on a small farm in Petaluma. Cliff Silliman was Ken's right-hand man in the Petaluma ministry.

One evening, Ken and Cliff invited me to come to Berachah House to help them pray for a man who needed deliverance from demonic spirits. We often prayed for people who had come out of occult backgrounds to receive deliverance. I was honored they wanted me to join them. I showed up eagerly for an assignment that proved to be more challenging than I had anticipated.

Ken, Cliff, and I met in one of the bedrooms so we could have privacy as we prayed. They gave me some information about the man we were going to pray for. Before long, they invited him into the room. I asked him some questions about his background. I wanted to know if he had been involved in the occult or had other experiences that might have opened his life to demonic spirits. After we talked for a few minutes, the three of us began to pray for him.

Very soon, all hell broke loose.

The man began to twitch and shake as he was being released from demonic spirits. At the same time, we heard loud shouting going on outside in the yard. I tried to ignore the shouting because the man we were praying for was experiencing important deliverance. I didn't want the distraction from the yard to interfere with this significant moment. As we were finishing up our prayer time, we heard a crash. The bedroom door burst open, and a man fell onto the floor at our feet.

Cliff stood up immediately, lifted the guy to his feet, and declared, "You're coming with me." As he started to lead the guy out of the room, I stopped him.

"No! He needs deliverance, too," I stated with authority. I figured he barged in because he was under demonic influence, and we should pray and set him free.

The man turned and looked at me. I stared into his eyes and demanded, "Demon, I command you to tell me your name!"

"My name is Bob! What's yours?" he yelled, as he lunged toward me, swinging his right arm and hitting me in the face. I fell back onto a couch with Bob on top of me. I hesitated to hit him back, remembering Jesus said to turn the other cheek. I also felt if I hit him, we would have a brutal fight.

Fortunately, Ken and Cliff grabbed him, pulled him off me, and dragged him out of the room. I sat stunned on the couch. A few minutes later, they came back and told me that Bob was drunk. He had been released from prison a few weeks earlier and was still a long way from being a mature disciple.

I apologized to Cliff for not allowing him to remove Bob when he first burst into the room. Ken and Cliff were the authorities when it came to the men on the farm. I learned a good lesson I have applied ever since. When I am visiting someone else's home or ministry, they are the ones in charge, not me.

Establishing Additional Discipleship Houses

Over the years, our Open Door churches had around twenty discipleship houses like Solid Rock in San Rafael, Novato, San Francisco, and Petaluma. We took in a lot of wild and crazy people. Many of them were transformed by the grace of God and the love of Christ in our fellowship. Others did not do well, either before meeting us, or after leaving us. Fortunately, the Lord protected us and our reputation as we ministered to these people.

The following is one of many stories of the Lord's work in these houses:

Bob and Diane Ellison had given a generous gift that enabled us to put a down payment on a sixteen-acre Christmas-tree farm with three houses in western Petaluma. Several acres of the land had been planted with pine and fir trees, which we harvested and sold for several years at Christmas time. Ken and Mary Sanders moved onto the farm, which they named *Thyatira*, after the church in the third chapter of Revelation.

A big, strong guy named David Murphy moved onto the farm. Dave came from a well-educated family in the Midwest. Once a drinker and barroom fighter, he had responded to Christ, and we offered him a place at Thyatira. Dave was a gifted carpenter, but he had trouble submitting to the authority of the men on the farm's construction crews. He and I became friends when I visited the ministries in Petaluma.

At a low point in his spiritual life, Dave went on a three-day fast. During his fast, he believed the Lord was directing him to go into the ministry. He enrolled in Golden Gate Seminary, then transferred to Princeton Seminary. After graduating, Dave moved to London and became the pastor of four small churches. He would preach at one church on Sunday morning and another on Sunday evening. The next week, he would preach at the third church on Sunday morning and the fourth on Sunday evening. Dave married a sweet lady named Lois, and their churches in London grew.

After several years in London, Dave and Lois moved back to America. Dave became the pastor of a Presbyterian church in Bellingham, Washington, which grew from a few hundred people to more than one thousand under his leadership.

A Much-Needed Vacation

As summer 1974 arrived, Kristina and I decided to get away for a vacation. It was our first trip away from Solid Rock since our honeymoon. We planned to spend a few days at Lighthouse Ranch, a large discipleship ministry in Eureka that was led by Jim Durkin.

On our drive to Eureka, I pulled over at a little country gas station to buy gas. As soon as I stopped the truck and opened the door, I heard a loud explosion, followed by a crash. Men were screaming somewhere in the back of the station.

To this day, the last thing I want is to see blood or to be near the scene of an accident. As a boy, I needed smelling salts to keep me from fainting when they drew my blood at the doctor's office.

However, I knew something terrible had just happened and I should help. I ran toward the back of the station, where I could hear men yelling. As I rounded the corner of the building, I saw two men running frantically through the garage in confusion. Another man was lying on his back on the floor of the garage. He was bleeding from a head wound.

I approached the man on the ground and saw that he had a huge gash on his forehead. I knelt beside him and yelled for someone to get me rags to stop the bleeding. He looked like he could die at any minute, so I started praying for him. One of the men brought me several rags. They seemed to be clean, so I began pressing them against his forehead. Someone was calling for an ambulance.

While I continued the compression, the fellow who brought me the rags told me what had happened. The man lying on the ground was a mechanic who worked at the gas station. He had been trying to force a rim back onto a big truck tire he had patched. The pressurized tire exploded as he was prying the rim on with a large crowbar. When it exploded, the rim shot skyward and gashed his forehead on its way up. It smashed through the ceiling and then fell back onto the ground. The wounded mechanic hit the cement floor.

It was forty-five minutes before an ambulance from the coast reached the gas station. I kept pressure on the injured mechanic's wound and kept praying for him the whole time. It was a tense scene that left me drained. I realized afterward the Lord can give us grace to do something in an emergency that we would never do under normal circumstances.

Once the ambulance arrived at the gas station, we continued

toward Eureka. I never knew whether the mechanic survived. It would be many years before Kristina and I would drive that winding road again.

Lighthouse Ranch

In Eureka, we spent three nights at Lighthouse Ranch. More than a hundred men and women who had been saved through the ministry of Gospel Outreach were living on this coastal ranch. They raised vegetables and had a few animals, but discipleship and outreach were the ministry's focus. The leader, Jim Durkin, was a man with a vision for training disciples and sending them out to the nations to preach the gospel.

I first heard about Jim when I went to the Festival of the Son in 1972. This festival was a gathering of a few thousand Jesus People from ministries throughout California as well as Oregon, Washington, and Alaska. The first festivals were held on a farm outside Santa Cruz where the ministries could bring their people and camp on the sloping hillside of the farm for three days of music and preaching.

These festivals were similar to music festivals from the '60s, except no one was smoking dope. Instead, we celebrated Jesus Christ who had delivered us from evil and filled us with the Holy Spirit.

Leaders from various ministries gave messages at morning and evening sessions. One of the most dynamic speakers was Jim Durkin. Jim was about six feet tall and weighed over 350 pounds. He struggled to move his big body around, but he loved the Lord and he could preach with power.

I was eager to visit Lighthouse Ranch to learn what I could from Jim's ministry. The ranch was on the Pacific coast. Its grassy fields were long and weedy, its barns and fences were old, and the weather was foggy. The hospitality of these believers was warm and friendly. They didn't know Kristina and me, and we had not told anyone we were coming for a visit, yet everyone we met welcomed us with hugs.

We ended up staying at the ranch with James and Lynn Jankoviak. They were a couple of years older than Kristina and me and had been given a house to live in by themselves. James was the editor of a paper published in Eureka. He loved to garden and had keen insights into the Kingdom of God. Lynn had been saved out of a hippie lifestyle. She had long, braided hair and wore flowered dresses. They fit right in with the California counterculture scene in 1974.

We returned to Solid Rock refreshed. Our lives changed again as we began the second year of our marriage.

CHAPTER TWENTY-TWO

BLESSINGS AHEAD

Expecting Again

A few months after returning from our trip to Eureka, we learned Kristina was pregnant again.

We were both happy, but this time we were more cautious about sharing the news. We wanted to make sure Kristina would carry the baby to full term. So, we made changes to our lifestyle to help ensure a successful pregnancy. Kristina modified her diet by eating more healthy foods, and she began taking vitamins. In addition, I was careful to not put extra pressure on her. I realized I needed to encourage her to sleep when she was tired and trust her to pace herself.

Kristina wanted to have a home birth. She had painful memories of being hospitalized for months in her early childhood years and wanted a more natural environment for the birth of our baby. We found Dr. Milton Estes, who had a great reputation for delivering babies at home.

I went with Kristina on her first visit to the doctor. We had a good talk about life and about the Lord. However, I became very uncomfortable when it was time for Dr. Estes to examine Kristina. He tried to reassure me that this was as natural for him as examining an ear, but I wasn't buying it. It wasn't until a few years later, when

I found out that Milton was gay, that I understood his explanation. By then, I knew he was a doctor I would recommend to any family having a home birth.

Kristina's New Job

In the spring of 1975, our ministry in Novato received a gift of $4,000 from the Steussy family. I knew just what I wanted to do with it. There were no Christian bookstores in Novato, and I felt sure that the Lord wanted us to open one.

I went into town and found a little red building, just off the main street. The phone number on the "For Rent" sign looked familiar. I called the number and was surprised when my uncle Lloyd Mason answered the phone. Lloyd was renting the building for $400 a month, which I quickly agreed to pay. This was the beginning of a fruitful, yet frustrating, business relationship Lloyd and I would have during the next eight years.

Returning home, I told Kristina I had a surprise gift for her. She asked if the gift was as big as our piano. I told her it was even bigger. Then she got excited. She thought I was buying her a car she really wanted. She was not as enthusiastic as I had hoped when I showed her the actual "present." I knew Kristina had the skills to manage our new store, but I didn't understand that a pregnant woman is more excited about giving birth to her baby than giving birth to a new ministry.

The bookstore began as a low budget, rinky-dink ministry. We had to stretch the money as far as possible because we did not have enough money to open a proper store. After tithing, then paying for a sign, the first and last months' rent, utilities, and miscellaneous expenses, Kristina was left with only $800 to buy books.

We decided to save money and build our own bookshelves. Barbara Brenoel, a widow in our church, donated a pile of plywood. A friend helped me cut the plywood into strips for bookshelves. We made little square boxes with some of the strips and put longer strips on the little boxes. Next, to spread out our meager inventory as much as possible, we placed a book, left two blank spaces, and then placed another book.

Kristina became the manager, the staff, and the janitor. In the following weeks, she was able to round up a few volunteers to assist her, and The Christian General Store in Novato was open for business. The word soon got out in the Christian community, and customers came from throughout the city.

As her pregnancy progressed, Kristina became exhausted easily. To compensate, she hung a bell on the store's door so she could lie down behind the counter and take naps until a customer walked through the door.

By the grace of God, our little store began to prosper.

Starting a Church

In June 1975, our ministry in Novato took another significant step. We had been bringing thirty to forty young people with us to the Church of the Open Door in San Rafael on Sunday mornings. Led by the Spirit, I asked permission from our pastors in San Rafael to start Sunday night services in Novato. After some intense discussion, they gave me their blessing.

The only affordable place I could find to hold Sunday night services was an abandoned bank building in Ignacio, two miles south of Novato. The property owners had other plans for the building and would only give us permission to rent it for a month. I was sure a lot could happen in a month, so I accepted their terms and we started services. The domed building could hold more than 300 people. The 25 people who showed up for our first service seemed swallowed up by the round room.

Nevertheless, I felt confident God would bless us, as He had ever since we began our ministry. At our first service I told the congregation that I could sense the day would come when this building would not be able to hold our entire church.

When the month was over, the owners extended our agreement. The Sunday night services in Ignacio went well. We grew slowly, and members of our congregation really loved one another.

A few months later, we were told we had to move. After some searching, the Lord provided us a new site—the city hall in downtown Novato. It was an old, red building with a creaky, wood floor, but it would work well for us. We were told we could have access to it for the next two weeks. With God's help, I knew a lot could happen in two weeks, so we made the move. One week led to the next, and we were able to use the building for the next few months.

After that, we had to start our building search again.

We were blessed when the Novato Episcopal Church offered to rent us their fellowship hall. We were told we could use it for the next three months. After our first two sites, three months sounded great. We accepted their offer and made the move. This ended up being our home for the next six months, until we were ready to take the next big step—Sunday morning services.

Matthew

Our first child was expected the first week of September. That spring, to make sure we were fully prepared for a home birth, Kristina signed us up for childbirth classes.

The classes taught the Bradley method of childbirth, which focused on deep breathing and emphasized the importance of the husband's role as a birth coach for his wife. I took the classes seriously. I even started doing extra pushups in case Kristina had back pain during labor that would need to be offset by me pushing on her back.

As her pregnancy progressed, Kristina grew very big. By the eighth month, she could rest her dinner plate on her protruding belly. One night, we were going to a party and she had put on her best maternity dress. "How do I look?" Kristina asked, as she turned sideways.

"You look like a camel," I replied as a halfhearted joke.

I should have known better. She broke into tears and refused to wear the dress. I told her I was sorry. I told her how beautiful she looked and how much I loved her. She calmed down, but I learned there is a time to joke and a time to keep my mouth shut with a pregnant wife.

By mid-September, Dr. Estes became concerned because Kristina was past her due date. He gave us the news that we would not be having a home birth after all. The baby's birth was now considered high risk. I knew childbirth could be dramatic, but we now started to experience trials we had not imagined.

The next day I was praying and felt an overwhelming love for Kristina and a great burden to pray for her safety during the birth. I realized she could die during the birth. She had scarlet fever as a child that damaged her heart. She had been warned by doctors to never have children. I sobbed deeply as I prayed and pleaded for her life and our baby's life. In hindsight, the Lord was allowing me to intercede in advance for a traumatic event that we would soon experience.

The baby was late . . . very late.

It wasn't until the end of September, or three weeks after her due date, that Kristina started having mild contractions. We went to see Dr. Estes. He checked her and said she was not dilating.

Finally, on October 1, Dr. Estes told us that we would have to schedule a Caesarean birth if Kristina's real labor had not started by the end of the week. In those days, if a woman had a Caesarean, then for safety's sake, all her subsequent births would need to be Caesarean. Also, it meant we could not have more than three children, since three C-sections were the most a woman could have without extreme danger.

We did not want a Caesarean birth. We were hoping to have more than three children someday, so we were feeling a lot of pressure.

On October 3, we decided to have a day of fasting and prayer. We appealed to the Lord to bring the baby quickly. Neither of us ate or drank anything except water all day. We fell asleep around 11:00 P.M. At midnight, Kristina woke me up with exciting news. Her water had broken, and her labor was in progress. I managed to go back to sleep, but the contractions kept her awake all night.

The next morning, we drove to Kentfield and checked into Marin General Hospital.

Kristina's labor went on all day, but she was not dilating the way she needed to. By evening, the hospital doctors were pressuring Dr. Estes to perform a Caesarean because there was a risk Kristina and the baby would be vulnerable to infection if her labor continued much longer.

I left the hospital room and started praying with intensity for the baby to come quickly. In my heart I still felt everything was fine. I had faith our baby would be born in God's perfect timing.

Kristina's labor went throughout the night. Her contractions went in cycles from mild to intense. When her contractions slowed down, she got out of bed and we walked the hospital corridors together, hoping it would stimulate her labor. Neither of us was able to sleep for more than a few minutes at a time. By the next morning, I was completely exhausted. However, Kristina was still not ready to give birth.

Meanwhile, the hospital doctors increased the pressure on Dr. Estes. They were trying to force him to perform a Caesarean.

By mid-morning, I left the room to find a quiet place to have some time with the Lord. I found a patio outside the hospital and knelt down to pray. The feelings of concern I had for Kristina and our baby during my prayer time a few weeks earlier came back stronger than ever. I cried out to the Lord to save my wife and our baby.

As I prayed, I remained convinced that Kristina did not need a Caesarean, but when I returned to the room, I learned that the doctors did not share my confidence. Medical prudence says that twenty-four hours after a pregnant woman's water has broken, the baby needs to be delivered as soon as possible, one way or another. By that afternoon, we were approaching forty hours and they wanted us to take a more aggressive approach.

After an X-ray showed there was nothing blocking the birth canal, we agreed to try one more thing before agreeing to a Caesarean birth. Kristina agreed to their recommendation to start taking Pitocin, a drug that induces strong contractions. They put a bag of it into her IV and we waited.

Within an hour her contractions became stronger than ever. It took four more hours of intense labor, along with another bag of Pitocin, before Kristina began to push the baby out.

Finally, at 1:00 A.M. on October 6, 1975, we saw the head of our baby appear. I stared in awe at the face of our child as he emerged from the birth canal. Moments later, our little boy was in my arms and I was weeping with joy and relief. I was overwhelmed with thankfulness to the Lord for the little guy and his health. I had feared that the drugs I had taken as a teenager might have caused damage to our baby.

Weeks earlier, we had picked names for both a boy and girl. The name we had chosen for a boy was Matthew. I loved the way the Gospel of Matthew was written. He recorded the words of Jesus beautifully, and I wanted to name our son after him. As tears poured down my face and I looked at our little boy for the first time, Dr. Estes asked me what his name was going to be. I couldn't answer him. As I looked at his face, I saw the spirit of the prophet Daniel. Daniel was a man of great wisdom and knowledge. I felt I could sense the destiny of our son. He would have the spirit of the prophet Daniel.

Nevertheless, we named our son Matthew. I knew it would cause Kristina too much consternation if I tried to change his name to Daniel without her prior consent.

Becoming a father was a joyous, life-changing experience. From the moment I first held Matthew, I felt the most powerful love I had ever experienced. I believed I would sacrifice my life for him if it were necessary.

Matthew looked healthy to me, but we discovered he had problems. He was jaundiced. His skin tone had an orange tinge, and he needed to be treated with ultraviolet lights in the hospital.

Two days after his birth, Kristina and I headed home without him. It was a strange feeling to drive home from the hospital and leave our baby behind. It would not be the last time our hearts were torn by having to leave Matthew in a hospital.

When we finally brought him home a few days later, he seemed to be doing fine. Kristina was nursing him and making sure she ate only healthy food.

A few months later, Matthew developed eczema over much of his body. We prayed for his healing and took him to the best doctors we could find. The doctors were not overly concerned, though they did say many babies who have eczema also develop asthma as they get older. This didn't concern us much at the time, because we did not understand the complications his asthma would bring into our lives.

As 1975 ended, I found myself not only the father of my first son, but also eager to start a new phase in our ministry—Sunday morning services for our Novato church.

PART SIX

GROWING THE FAITH AND THE FAMILY

CHAPTER TWENTY-THREE

NEW PHASE OF MINISTRY

Launching Sunday Morning Services

As 1976 began, I was eager to move forward with plans for Sunday morning services in Novato. We had 50 committed people attending our Sunday-night services, and 40–50 coming to Tuesday night Bible studies. New people were also coming to our Christian General Store all the time, seeking ministry and direction, along with books and music. I began to believe God was calling me to gather these people into a church family.

The pastors in San Rafael initially resisted my idea. Dick Bruener was leading the ministries in San Francisco, and Ken Sanders was leading the ministries in Petaluma. They also had prosperous bookstores, Bible studies, and discipleship houses. However, our pastors didn't feel the time was right for any of us to launch Sunday morning services yet.

I was disappointed, but I did not challenge this decision. I believed in submitting to the authority of the pastors I worked with in San Rafael. I felt the Lord would move on their hearts and I would move forward when the time was right.

At the same time, good things continued to happen in our Bible studies. Every Tuesday night, we packed people into the clubhouse at the Parkhaven Apartments in Novato. We would sing, pray, and share testimonies. I would then give a Bible teaching followed by an invitation for people to commit their lives to Christ. Without fail, every week, several new people would make first-time decisions to follow Jesus.

Hylan and Rita

I first met Hylan and Rita Slobodkin at one of our Sunday morning services in San Rafael. Like many of the new people who came to our services, I had no idea if I would ever see them again. I found out they lived in Novato, and I invited them to join our Tuesday night Bible study at the Parkhaven clubhouse.

It turned out, Hylan and Rita became two of the most significant people in our lives. They were a Jewish couple from Los Angeles. They did not fit the mold of typical new believers. They lived on a small communal farm with other hippies in Novato. Prior to this, in 1970, they had opened their hearts to Christ at L'Abri, the community established by Christian philosopher Francis Schaeffer and his wife, Edith, in Switzerland. After four months at L'Abri, they had traveled to Israel and lived on a kibbutz for a year.

In Israel, Hylan fell away from the Lord and began to live the life of a hippie once again. Hylan had a long beard, and his brown hair was down to his waist. Rita was short and sweet, with black hair. Her face radiated a beautiful smile, and her faith was alive. They sat on the floor in the middle of the Bible study and sometimes hugged and kissed while I was teaching.

One Tuesday night, Rita raised her hand and asked me to explain how I felt about smoking marijuana. It didn't take the gift of discernment to realize that she wanted me to help Hylan get the message, so he would quit smoking weed. I made the dangers of marijuana clear, but Hylan had a stubborn streak. He was against nuclear power, the chemicals in ice cream, and meat, but pro marijuana.

A few weeks later, I preached from Luke 8:21, where Jesus said, "My mother and brothers and sisters are those who hear the word of God and do it." When I gave the invitation to accept Jesus as Lord and Savior, Hylan stood up to recommit his life to Christ. He never turned back again.

Kristina and I invited the Slobodkins over for dinner one Sunday after our services. She prepared salmon and salad. After some intense discussion, Hylan and Rita, who had been vegetarians, ate the first meat they had tasted in years. About that time, Hylan went out one night at their little farm and poisoned the marijuana growing in their garden. He was taking his faith seriously.

A Fulltime "Priest"

In May 1976, I again brought up the idea of spinning off our Novato ministries into our own church. This time the idea was received favorably and in a bigger way than I had anticipated. Our San Rafael pastors decided to plant three new Open Door churches at the same time by launching the Open Door ministries in Novato, San Francisco, and Petaluma into new churches on the second Sunday of June.

On the first Sunday of June, we invited Dr. Dubois, the professor of missions and evangelism at Golden Gate Seminary in Mill Valley, to speak at our last combined service in San Rafael. On the next Sunday, we had four separate Open Door churches in four cities. Our little movement had taken a big step. We had no idea of the fruitfulness these churches would produce, nor could we anticipate the challenges they would face in the years to come.

Our church, the Church of the Open Door Novato, was launched with weekly Sunday morning services in the Masonic Building. We started with fifty people on the first Sunday and grew a little every week. Tom Wise was our worship leader. Brad Friedlander was our associate pastor, and many in the congregation volunteered their services from day one.

As our congregation grew, I was given a raise that enabled me to stop doing construction work and concentrate all my energies on the ministry. I had now gone from being a hippie to a full-time evangelical "priest". At least, I hoped the Lord considered me a legitimate priest. I felt once we started the church, I would be committed for as long as it took for it to develop into a healthy, thriving fellowship. Between my salary of $1,200 a month from the church and the rent paid by the others living at Solid Rock, we just made it financially every month.

CHAPTER TWENTY-FOUR

LEARNING AND GROWING

I put in a lot of time in prayer and sermon preparation each week. My normal ministry schedule included preaching Sunday mornings, teaching Bible studies both Sunday and Tuesday nights, and leading our elders meetings on Mondays.

I began teaching a weekday Bible study at Fireman's Fund Insurance Company in San Rafael, where several of our people worked. In addition, I was reading four chapters in the Old Testament and another four chapters in the New Testament every day for personal devotions.

We also hosted frequent leadership meetings in our home and had Pat McCornack, Steve Brown, and Merilee Rosie living with us at Solid Rock.

In spite of the time I spent with the Lord, I began to show signs of burnout, though I didn't recognize it at the time. Burnout happens when we give out more energy each week than we can recoup. Eventually, something starts to give. I pushed myself hard, and I expected a lot from everyone who served the Lord with me.

Head of Household

Kristina's responsibilities included caring for our son,

242 FROM DARKNESS INTO LIGHT

Matthew, as well as managing the food, bills, shopping, and chores for our family and Solid Rock. She also oversaw the Christian General Store in Novato. After keeping this pace for a while, Kristina made it clear she felt neglected. I got the message after she asked me several times to read H. Page Williams's book, *Do Yourself a Favor: Love Your Wife.*

I eventually read a few chapters and found a section that explained that husbands were the head of the house and should run the family finances. I marched the book over to Kristina and showed her the chapter. I then insisted on taking over our family checkbook. She didn't like the idea. She is a gifted bookkeeper and I'm a busy guy who doesn't like details. However, she relented.

A few weeks later, after I had bounced a couple of checks, I walked over to where Kristina was sitting. "I'm the head of the house, right?" I demanded. She nodded, skeptically. Without hesitation I added sheepishly, "I command that you take care of our finances from now on."

We have not bounced another check since.

Praying and Fasting for the United States

I was never completely content to simply be a pastor in a suburban community. I love our country and was concerned about our political and moral condition. I wanted to help shape our nation.

July 4, 1976 was America's bicentennial, our nation's 200th birthday. A group called Intercessors for America put out a newsletter addressing key issues facing America. They also encouraged Christians all over our country to fast and pray for our nation on the first Friday of every month.

I joined those Friday fasts, along with thousands of others around the country. It was difficult for me to wake up on those Friday mornings knowing that I wasn't going to eat or drink anything except water until I woke up again on Saturday morning. When I got hungry, I tried to remember the seriousness of the moral and spiritual issues facing America. I often prayed that God would send a revival to our nation. I was never in the military defending our country, but I felt like fasting and prayer allowed me to make a contribution in the spiritual war our nation fights.

No matter how powerful or prosperous we are, if we lose our spiritual foundation, we will end up captive and enslaved to sin. Sin and deception have serious consequences.

In those days, once or twice a week, I would go into the hills in Novato to pray. I would often hike until I found a spot with a nice shade tree and a view of the valley below. I would pray for God to bless our city as well as our nation. I liked to sing aloud and declare praises to the Lord who had saved me. I was never a good singer, but I knew the Lord didn't care whether or not I could carry a tune. It was liberating to worship and sing with joy before the Lord.

Moving to Bigger Facilities

Our church was growing and our family was healthy as 1976 came to an end.

The Lord was prospering our Christian General Store as well. As the year ended, we moved our bookstore around the corner, from my uncle Lloyd's tiny red building to a bigger storefront he also owned on Grant Avenue.

244 FROM DARKNESS INTO LIGHT

When the store moved, we also rented an apartment above the store for the church. The little apartment was my first office. I put my desk in the only bedroom, and we put a couch and chairs in the little living room. The tap water in the apartment was so bad, if you set a glass of water down for a few minutes, rust would accumulate in the bottom of the glass. There were also termites in the building. When Lloyd dropped by one day, I pointed to a spot outside where termites were burrowing into the eaves. He looked at the termites and observed, "It takes a long time for termites to finish off a building."

Obviously, we were not a high-budget operation. Our family and our church paid every bill on time, but we had no savings. However, early in 1977, to accommodate our continued growth, we moved our Sunday services from the Masonic Building into a new Boys Club on Wilson Avenue in Novato.

Mom's Admonition: "Don't Ever Do That Again!"

I was still learning a lot about ministry. I was doing five teachings each week, along with handling the challenges of daily pastoral ministry. The challenge of coming up with fresh teachings each week caught up with me one Sunday and taught me a lesson.

I had heard preachers declare, "If the Lord doesn't give me something to preach, I won't be saying anything at all." I believed that would never happen to me. I always prayed and asked the Lord to guide me, and the Holy Spirit always prompted me or opened up specific scriptures, so I would have an edifying message for our congregation.

One week, I had a different experience. I had been busy as

usual but still spent time praying and thinking about my message. I searched many scriptures to see if there was something the Lord wanted me to emphasize. Absolutely nothing came to me all week. On Sunday morning, I woke up feeling nervous but was still expecting a message to be revealed to me. After arriving at the Boys Club, I prayed with our leaders before the service, still assuming that, at any minute, the Lord would show me His plan. I greeted our members and guests as several hundred people, including my mother, filed in for the service. It was special to have my mom come since she usually attended St. Isabella's Catholic Church.

I didn't tell anyone I didn't have a message to preach. Still hoping for the Lord's revelation, I told Tom Wise to take his time leading the worship. Tom was surprised since I was always concerned about how much time each part of the service took. So, we sang, and then I led us in prayer and communion. Still, no message came to me.

I asked if anyone in the church had a testimony to share. A couple of people walked up to the stage and I handed them the microphone. They spoke for a few minutes each. Their testimonies were OK but not memorable. They sat down, and I went back up and asked if anyone else had a testimony. One more lady came up and shared something precious to her but not too edifying to the rest of us.

I asked Tom to lead us in a couple more songs and then I closed the service with prayer. I tried to put on a good face as I greeted people after the service, but my smile is not very big, even when I'm happy. I went up to my mom and asked, "What did you think of the service today?"

She looked me in the eye and declared, "Mark, don't ever do that again."

By the grace of God, I've never had to do that again.

CHAPTER TWENTY-FIVE

CHALLENGES AND TRIALS

Money Problems

It never occurred to me that we would have financial problems as we followed the Lord. But, in early 1977, for the first time since I was a child, I was completely out of money.

I had literally put my last five dollars into an offering when I went to a meeting led by a couple who were healing evangelists. They had told everyone God would bless us a hundredfold if we gave generously to their ministry. I didn't believe their claims, but I assumed the Lord would still take care of me. I thought about the deal I felt the Lord had given me seven years earlier on the bank of the Truckee River. I believed as long as I served God with my entire heart, He would take care of my financial needs. For six years, construction or painting jobs had always come when I needed them. When I stopped doing construction work, our finances became very tight.

My salary from the church covered our share of the rent, food, and utilities. However, recent car repairs had emptied our checking account. I did have an idea. I went to my mom's house with the only possessions that I could easily sell, besides my truck. I sold my .22 rifle to my brother Robert for $20. I also sold my shotgun to my brother Barry for $100. I told Robert and Barry to take good care of the guns because I hoped to buy them back someday.

I was no longer completely broke, but my options were slim. The $120 covered our gas, food, and other needs for the next two weeks.

The more I thought about my situation, the calmer I became. Technically, I didn't have any cash, but our real needs were being met. We had paid every bill on time, and we were still eating well. I just didn't have any money or credit cards in my wallet.

One day, soon after the $120 was gone, I went to our mailbox and took out our mail. There was some junk mail as well as an envelope addressed to me. I didn't recognize the handwriting, and there was no return address. When I opened the envelope, I discovered a five-dollar bill folded inside a plain piece of paper. There was no letter or note of explanation.

I used that five dollars to put gas in my truck. A week later, another envelope addressed to me arrived. Inside it was another five dollars. Week after week, some precious person sent me five dollars.

Within a few months, our finances improved. Our church was growing, and I got a raise. About the same time, the five-dollar envelopes ceased. To this day, I have no idea who sent them to me, but I will always be thankful for that person's generosity when we were broke.

Prayers and Fasting

As spring arrived, a missionary came to speak at our Sunday night service. He talked about mission's work in Turkey and what God was doing in several foreign countries. As he spoke, I realized

God was working powerfully around the world in ways I knew nothing about.

I didn't feel called to be a missionary, but I felt compelled to do something to further God's kingdom in foreign countries. I felt challenged to fast and pray for a different nation each week. I didn't want to take up this challenge on my own, so I decided to ask a few men at the church if they would join me in weekly fasting and prayer.

Mike Griffiths, John Rucker, Hylan Slobodkin, Sev Morrison, Jack Straw, and others rotated into our group each week, joining me each Friday for prayer at 6:00 P.M. in my office above the Christian General Store. We used a book titled *Operation World* to help us focus on the prayer needs of the country for which we were praying each week. *Operation World* gave statistics about the spiritual condition of every nation.

The first few months were difficult when we gathered for prayer. The guys came to the meeting hungry and weary from working all day. We prayed with difficulty for those we didn't know and would probably never see. At the same time, we started to share personal concerns for prayer, along with Bible verses that were meaningful to each of us.

During the third month, the meeting dynamics changed one Friday night. Several of us were kneeling while others lay face down on the carpet as we prayed. As different men were praying from their hearts, I sensed the presence of the Holy Spirit in the room in a new and powerful way. The self-consciousness that often accompanies men praying in a group setting was gone.

Each man, in his own way, was expressing the true concerns

of his heart in his prayers. There was no sense that anyone was dominating the meeting, nor was anyone being left out. The Holy Spirit was enabling us to pray and intercede with freedom and unity. Once this breakthrough occurred, our group had a more powerful dynamic than ever before. I began to look forward to Fridays each week. Our meetings were like a gathering of an underground cell of spiritual warriors. We didn't have much money or positions of influence, but we knew we were connecting with the Lord in a way none of us had ever experienced before.

We eventually enriched our friendships by changing our fasting schedule. Originally, we fasted from the time we woke up on Friday morning until the time we woke up on Saturday morning. We changed the schedule to start our fast after lunch on Thursday and ended the fast after our meeting ended on Friday night. This allowed us to have dinner together on many Friday nights. These dinners were like victory celebrations. Our hearts were full of grace, and the food tasted especially good after our fasts.

CHAPTER TWENTY-SIX

OUR GROWING FAMILY

Fatherhood

In May 1977, Kristina gave me the good news that she was pregnant again. We made an appointment with Dr. Estes and told him we were hoping for a home birth this time. We also planned to scale back Solid Rock to the four of us, with no more than two or three others. We wanted to be surprised by the gender of our coming baby, so we didn't look at the ultrasound results.

About this time, I learned a lesson in my role as Matthew's father that I've never forgotten.

Matthew was strong-willed and often tested us. The only thing he responded to in some situations was a spanking, which had usually been quick and painful enough to have the desired effect on him.

When Matthew was two-and-a-half years old, he started developing a bad habit. We would put him to bed, and a few minutes later, he would climb out of his crib and come into our bedroom. He had been fed and prayed for. He was tired, and it was time to go to sleep, but he would not stay in his crib. I was firm and clear with him about staying in bed and going to sleep, but night after night, he got out of bed and came into our room anyway.

I knew he was testing my resolve, and I spanked him for being disobedient. However, spanking did not work in this situation. He still showed up in our bedroom every night after crawling out of his crib. After our battle of wills went on a few weeks, I was feeling like a horrible father. I loved Matthew and didn't want to continue spanking him.

One night, Kristina and I put Matthew into his crib at bedtime and told him to go to sleep. We had fed him, prayed with him, and followed our usual futile routine. We then went into our room and lay down on our bed. A few minutes later, our bedroom door slowly opened. Once again, Matthew was standing in our room. I picked him up firmly and carried him into his room, to put him back to bed. As I stood over his crib, I got an idea. Instead of issuing a warning or spanking, I sat down on a chair with him in my arms and looked him in the eye.

"Matthew, I'm going to tell you a story. It's a true story. When it's over, I want you to go to sleep." He looked at me with his big blue eyes. He understood me perfectly.

I began, "A long, long time ago, in the nation of Babylon, there was a man named Daniel who loved the Lord very much. . . ." I told Matthew the story of "Daniel and the Lions' Den" with all the passion I could muster. Even though I hate scary movies, I made this story as scary as possible. The saliva was dripping off the mouths of those lions!

Matthew listened, wide-eyed, to the entire story. He laughed when I pretended to throw him into a lions' den and showed no fear of the hungry lions. At the end of the story, I picked him up, hugged him, prayed a blessing over him, and put him in his crib. Then, I headed for our bedroom.

I lay down on our bed as usual and waited with Kristina for our bedroom door to open. After ten minutes, I began to wonder where Matthew was. After fifteen minutes, I had a faint sense of hope. I got up and walked quietly toward his room, opened his door, and looked into his crib. He was fast asleep. I could barely believe it.

The next night at bedtime I told him the story of Daniel and the Lions' Den again. I told it with the same passion and all the detail. We then prayed together, and I headed to our bedroom. I waited awhile and then crept back into Matthew's bedroom. He was sound asleep.

After a week of "Daniel and the Lions' Den" every bedtime, I asked Matt if he would like a different story. He didn't want a different one. So, I kept retelling the story, and he kept going right to sleep every night. After two weeks, I insisted on telling him the story of David and Goliath. He got all the gory details, including David cutting off the giant's head with his sword. He loved it.

In the weeks and months that followed, he heard about Jonah and the huge fish, Shadrach, Meshach, and Abednego, and Samuel. I would read over the stories in advance to get insights and details. When the king's guards were throwing the Hebrew boys into the fiery furnace, I would pick Matthew up, pretend to tie him up, and then throw him onto the far side of the bed. He would laugh and want to do it over and over again.

Bedtime became our special time together. He looked forward to the stories and our prayer times. I loved telling Bible stories to him and praying with him every night. I continued to study the

Bible for details that would help the stories come alive. I'm sure it helped my preaching to the church as well, and Matthew never got out of bed before morning again.

Personal Heartache

I wish I could say I had discovered the key to having all my prayers answered in ways more wonderful than I had imagined. My experience has been more complex than that. When God answers prayers in a powerful way, it is wonderful. However, we our faith can be tested when our heartfelt prayers are not answered in the way we hope or expect.

At a time when many wonderful things were happening in our church and ministries, one thing close to our hearts was very troubling. When he was two years old, Matthew contracted severe asthma.

Kristina had nursed Matthew, and we fed him fruit and vegetables every day. We investigated every known remedy to help him overcome allergies. Kristina took him to numerous doctors. Our friends and church leaders joined us in prayer for his healing many times. Yet, nothing seemed to help him get better.

By the time he was four years old, Matthew started waking up wheezing every night. His skin would turn blue from lack of oxygen. We often put him in a hot shower to help him breathe. We would give him his inhaler and rub his back as we prayed for him to get his breath. He couldn't run without wheezing when he played outside. He was so thin that his ribs protruded on both sides.

As he got older, his condition grew slowly worse, regardless of what we tried to do to help him. Kristina and I loved him with all our hearts. It was crushing us to see him suffer.

Philip

On the evening of February 9, 1978, I went with my friend Russ Dillon to play pool in downtown Novato. Kristina had been experiencing some minor contractions, so I gave her the phone number at the pool hall in case she went into labor. Russ and I were in a tight match when Kristina phoned and asked me to come right home.

I hurried back and learned that her labor was going strong. An hour later, the midwife and Dr. Estes came over, and Kristina's labor intensified. We were excited to have a home birth, but that night we got a reality check about the dangers of giving birth at home.

Kristina went through labor on our bed. It seemed like she was sprinting uphill carrying a thirty-pound bag, which was kicking its way out of her abdomen. Four hours from the start of this marathon, she began to push the baby out. After the prolonged labor she went through with Matthew's birth, this seemed to happen really fast.

Everything was going well until our baby's head emerged. I looked at the baby's dark face. As soon as Kristina made one final push, Dr. Estes grabbed our baby boy, who was dark blue. I knew by the doctor's reaction that something was wrong. He didn't pause for me to cut the umbilical cord, he did it himself. He was all business and moving fast. He asked his nurse for his suction tubes and she handed him a jar with two tubes coming out of it. He put one tube into the baby's mouth and down into his lungs. He began to suck on the end of the other tube.

Our baby boy had begun to breathe inside the womb and had inhaled the meconium fluid inside the placenta. A baby with meconium aspiration can suffer brain damage because his lungs get clogged and he can't get oxygen. Dr. Estes continued to suck on the tube and the cup began to fill with thick black fluid. The nurse was tending to Kristina, and I was praying for our son. After five agonizing minutes, Dr. Estes paused, and our little boy began to breathe. Kristina and I started thanking God and crying with relief.

Once it was clear that he was going to be okay, I held our new son for the first time. As I gazed at the chunky, ten-pound fellow, I saw the spirit of the Apostle Peter in him. The Lord was showing me that he was destined to be a leader. We named him Philip after my grandmother Cicely's brother, who died when he was a young boy.

Philip had jaundice, just like Matthew. His blood was also too thick. We set up fluorescent lights in our bedroom and let him bask in the glow so his body would be able to process the jaundice. Two days later, we took him to the hospital, where they let him be a blood donor so his circulatory system would be in proper balance.

If Dr. Estes had not come to the birth with the right equipment to clear his lungs, Philip would have either died or been brain damaged. We chose to have our babies at home because we had hoped for natural, calm childbirths in a relaxed atmosphere. There was nothing relaxing about the birth of either of our boys. But, by the grace of God, they survived.

Within a couple of weeks, Philip was doing great. Kristina was nursing him, and I had recovered from being an emotional wreck.

Before long, Philip joined Matthew for our bedtime Bible

story time. I propped him up on a pillow next to Matthew. He, too, was tied up and thrown into the lions' den, the fiery furnace, or the raging sea, night after night. I told the boys that someday I wanted them to tell these stories to their own children.

CHAPTER TWENTY-SEVEN

OUTREACH

Broadcasting the Word

The cable television company in Novato offered four TV channels to our community.

Then in 1977, the company opened a community service channel, which was used to broadcast the Novato City Council meetings. The cable company had one camera that panned across the room and focused on the council members as they discussed the issues of our city each week. I found myself watching the City Council proceedings several times.

Our experience of the Holy Spirit's presence in our Friday-night fasting and prayer meetings was so powerful that we wanted the entire world to know about the love of God. In our prayer sessions, we began asking the Lord to open doors for us to preach the gospel around the world. I specifically prayed for opportunities to preach on radio and television.

As we prayed those bold prayers week after week, I started thinking about the local cable television station. I wondered if we could use the station like the City Council was doing. Every time I considered the practicality of it, I dropped the idea, because we had very little money, influence, or understanding about television.

Then, some encouraging things happened.

First, I was invited to be interviewed on a television program on a major station in San Francisco. The program was hosted by a Catholic priest who was a friend of Father John O'Conner, our family friend. He had recommended that the host invite me as a guest.

When I got to the station for my first live television program, I was impressed with the simplicity of the interview. We sat in chairs facing each other and talked like two friends in a living room. The cameramen videotaped our conversation, and the studio broadcast it to thousands of viewers. It was a simple way to speak to a lot of people at once.

Second, I had a conversation with Chuck, a member of our church who worked for the local cable TV company. I asked him how the City Council made the arrangements to have their meetings aired. He told me the station made television time available to the public at no cost. When I asked him about the possibility of our church having a program on the station, he encouraged me to drop by the station and talk to the general manager.

While I was excited about the possible opportunity, I was also intimidated by the challenges and felt inadequate. It took months for me to get the courage to show up at the cable company. Sometimes, it is difficult to believe that God will actually accomplish the things we ask him to do when we pray.

One day, I decided that I had nothing to lose. It was time to find out if the breakthroughs I felt were happening in our prayer meetings would produce tangible results. That afternoon, I dressed up and drove downtown to the cable company. I walked through the door of their storefront office and met the receptionist.

"How can I help you?" she asked as I stood trembling in her presence.

"I was hoping to talk to someone about the possibility of putting a program on the air," I replied.

"You need to talk to our general manager. Just a moment, please."

Picking up the phone, she asked the general manager if he was available to talk with me. She put down the phone, pointed to the door beside her, and informed me, "He's right in there."

As I opened the door, I saw a man behind a simple office desk with only a couple of papers and a phone on it.

Extending my hand to him, I introduced myself. "Hello, I'm Mark Buckley, the pastor of the Open Door Christian Church."

He shook my hand in reply and responded, "Take a seat. How can I help you?"

My heart was beating rapidly. This was a humble office with a nice guy in front of me, but I felt the weight of our prayers and hopes riding on our conversation..

"I've seen the City Council meetings on your cable station, and I was wondering if it would be possible for our church to put a program on your station." I was so nervous my voice was squeaking.

"Sure! How many days a week do you have in mind?"

He caught me off-guard. I had not even considered we could be on more than once a week, but I decided to take a chance and step out big.

"Two or three times a week would be great, if that were possible."

"OK. What time would you like to be on?"

I hadn't given a moment's thought to what time of day we would want our program to be on the air. I was scrambling in my mind and decided to ask for prime time.

"Well, 7:00 or 7:30 P.M. would be great, if that is open," I suggested.

"Okay, we will go for 7:30 Monday, Wednesday, and Friday evenings. Just drop off your videotapes at our front desk and we will put them on the air. Anything else I can do for you?"

"No, that is great. Thank you very much." I shook hands with him and left the office feeling like I was walking on a cloud.

As I got into my car, I couldn't wait to tell the guys in our prayer group what had happened. I kept thinking about how intimidated I had been about asking for this opportunity. Most likely, the door had been wide open the entire time. It seemed like they were just waiting for someone to ask permission to put programs on the air.

When I got home, I phoned my friend Terry, the pastor of The Church on the Hill in Vallejo, and asked him if we could use the recording equipment his church had for broadcasting their Sunday services. He told me we would have to pay his studio engineer and cameramen, but they would probably be glad to work for us.

In the following weeks, we assembled a team of eager amateurs to tape our programs. Patty Stockton was our producer. She lined up guests for interviews and musicians to sing. Randy McKie was trained as our cameraman, and Hylan Slobodkin became our production editor.

On the first Saturday morning, we packed chairs and a coffee table from our living room into my truck. We put a curtain on a frame for a backdrop and drove over to Vallejo. We taped three programs at The Church on the Hill. In each, I interviewed leaders in our church and asked them to share testimonies about what God had done in their lives.

Production costs were $500 for the three programs. That paid for their cameramen and director, as well as use of the church facility in Vallejo for production. Our cable company put the programs on the air the following Monday, Wednesday, and Friday for free.

The next Sunday in our worship service at the Boys Club, I asked a visitor how she found out about us. She told me she had seen our program on TV. We were off and running.

As time went by, we expanded the program's reach by simply making copies of the tapes and dropping them off at cable stations in San Francisco and in the East Bay. The programs blessed many viewers and gave several people an opportunity to minister on television for the first time in their lives. In the years to come, these programs would impact our ministry in more ways than I could have imagined.

I experienced the reality that when we trust God, He has the power to open doors and bring our hopes and dreams to pass.

International Expansion

One spring afternoon, about fifteen pastors from the four Open Door churches came to our house for a leadership meeting. We were all reading *Spiritual Leadership* by J. Oswald Sanders. This outstanding book challenges leaders to seek and serve the Lord with excellence. After discussing a few chapters, we started talking about our future missions and outreach.

There was a spirit of unity among the men as we shared our vision with one another. We discussed starting a church in Mexico City and another one in London. We knew if we could establish fruitful churches in those two cities, we could touch much of the world. Both of those capitals are hubs with networks into many nations and cultures. The universities in London draw students from Africa, the Middle East, and India. The universities in Mexico City educate students from Central and South America. We became excited about these possibilities. We assumed we would face challenges, but we agreed we had to try to fulfill this vision.

The following month, Kent, Ken Sanders, and I went to San Francisco to meet with Dick Bruener at his home. Kent felt we needed an organization to help formalize our relationship as churches. He felt this would keep our churches from drifting apart. We agreed with him. Also, with plans to start mission churches in the future, we felt setting up a missionary corporation would help serve both purposes.

We called our new organization the Open Door Commission [ODC]. Each of our churches would contribute a portion of their church tithes, and we would use the funds to support new Open Door church plants. We started meeting together once a month as leaders of the ODC.

London

Kristina was six months pregnant when she and I took a trip to London in November 1977. Our assignment was to determine the feasibility of starting an Open Door church in England. We planned to meet with believers Kent knew in London and scout out the land.

Kent's friend Gerard was supposed to meet us at Heathrow Airport when we arrived. After our eleven-hour flight from San Francisco, we walked through Heathrow airport keeping our eyes open for Gerard. We knew he was a German about our age, but we didn't know what he looked like.

When I spotted a bearded man with freckles who was searching the crowd walking through the airport, I stopped to ask if he was looking for someone from America. He was an Englishman of Irish descent, and he wasn't looking for us. Nevertheless, we started talking with him and found out his name was Roy Hendy. Roy worked for the Customs Department at Heathrow. He loved the Lord, and I felt an immediate connection with him.

Roy gave us his phone number and told us to come by and visit him and his family if we had time. I put his phone number in my wallet and forgot about it when Gerard showed up a few minutes later. I didn't realize at the time that this had been a divine appointment. Roy would become my most significant contact in London.

We spent the next ten days in London with Gerard and his wife, Karen. We met many believers who were friends of Kent, and some who knew David Hoyt, another leader in the Jesus Movement. We walked through the rain and fog and saw the sights of the city. Taking Kristina to the Tower of London, Big Ben, and Buckingham Palace renewed my memories of my earlier travels with my grandmother. Visiting these places with my wife, sharing old memories and creating new ones, was delightful.

After we had visited with all the contacts on our list, we still had a few days left before flying home. I remembered Roy Hendy and decided to give him a call. Roy immediately invited us to his home in Slough, just outside London. We took a train to Slough, where Roy, his wife, June, and their five children greeted us. Over the next two days, we heard Roy's testimony. He had been an alcoholic for many years. He was frustrated with his wife and alienated from his children. One day, Roy met a young American man at Heathrow Airport who needed a place to stay. Roy invited him to stay with his family. Roy did not realize the young man was an evangelist. Over the next few days, he led Roy's children to Christ.

Once the Hendy children gave their hearts to the Lord, they started to forgive their dad and pray for him. As Roy saw the transformation in his children, it melted his heart. Soon, he and June also committed their lives to Christ. As they began to share their faith with their friends, several others committed their lives to Christ as well.

Some new believers were living with Roy and June and their five children when we came to visit. They invited me to speak to the weekly prayer meeting held in their living room. By the time we left two days later, the Hendys were true friends in Christ. They soon named their ministry, "The House of the Open Door Community."

We loved the believers we met in London and saw great potential in starting a church in the city. When we got back home, however, I knew we shouldn't plan to move. Kristina had major reservations about whether Matthew could handle the cold, damp climate with his asthma. I also had concerns about who would take over leadership in the Novato church. We reported back to the Open Door pastors that a church plant in London was a great idea, but someone else was going to have to lead it. The Open Door Commission funded two teams in the next year to plant churches. The first team was led by the Anderson and Smith families, whom we sent to Mexico City. The other team was comprised of the Hoffman and Hoyt families, whom we sent to London. Both teams were led by competent pastors from the Church of the Open Door in San Rafael.

They were eager to go and establish churches, but none of us realized the trials they were going to face in the months ahead.

Spreading the Word

In the winter of 1978, I gathered a group of people from our church who were interested in helping launch an in-house magazine. I wanted the magazine to include teachings from our leaders, testimonies from our members, and cartoons from our artists. The six people who met in our living room included a Stanford graduate who majored in English, an artist, and three writers. I told them I would contribute articles but wanted them to be in charge of the magazine's publication and production. I cautioned them that our resources were limited. We would need to start simply and build the magazine month by month.

I left that first meeting early because I wanted the group to select a leader and make production plans without me. They continued to meet for another hour and scheduled another meeting for a week later. I was eager to see what they would come up with in the days to come. After a month had gone by, I asked the artist how the magazine was progressing. He gave me a report that concerned me. The plan he shared with me was for a publication that sounded like it was going to be a Christian version of *TIME* magazine. It was so extravagant that none of them had the capacity to pull it off. They felt overwhelmed by the task and didn't have another meeting scheduled.

Reconvening the group a few weeks later, I honored the work they had done in my absence but explained how we were going to go forward more simply. In two weeks, we would gather whatever articles and artwork we had, give it to my secretary, and she would have it printed. Our little magazine would be so simple that people would look at it and say, "This is nice, but I can do better than that." Whoever thought they could do a better job than we were doing would be recruited to help us with our next edition.

We published the first edition of *Son Life* two weeks later. Every month, our little magazine had new features. We added interviews, upgraded the printing quality, and wrote better teaching articles as we went along. *Son Life* never made a huge impact, but it was a blessing just the same. It enabled many of our members to contribute something that touched our church and those on our mailing list.

As the magazine grew in circulation and quality, my articles focused on the principles of how God works in my life:

• The Lord gives me a vision for something and expects me to go forward one step at a time. I rarely have the finances and other resources to pull off the vision that's in my heart when I first start a ministry.

• We start small and grow slowly, until the ministry resembles what the Lord originally put in my heart. If I were to wait until I had all the resources necessary, I would not have started our church, our bookstore, or much of anything else.

• People with gifts and resources join me as I go along. Their vision and gifts enhance and adjust my vision. They make the ministry greater than I ever could on my own. Together, we do a ministry that is fruitful and brings glory to God.

The Stocktons

One spring day, I came into my office just after noon and found a note from our bookstore manager: *A Dr. Stockton stopped by and asked if we knew of any houses for rent for his family. He will come by again later.* The note seemed odd to me. I wondered what kind of doctor goes into a Christian bookstore looking for a house for his family.

I soon found out. An hour later, there was a knock on the door, and I invited the doctor to come into my office. I had no way of knowing this would be one of the most significant encounters of my life.

Fortunately, I had some free time and ended up talking with Dr. Glen (Billy) Stockton for more than an hour that afternoon. I asked why he was looking for a house, and then asked him to tell me about his life and his walk with the Lord. Billy was twenty-eight years old, just a few months older than me. He had three younger sisters, his mother loved the Lord, and his father was a colonel in the Air Force. The family had lived on Air Force bases around the country, finally settling in Tucson, Arizona.

Billy had lived a wild life from his late teen years until he married Patty at the age of twenty-three. Patty loved the Lord and helped Billy return to the faith his mother had taught him as a child. He was working as a fireman in Tucson, when he and Patty had three boys, one right after another.

At that point, Billy decided to become a doctor and was admitted into the University of Arizona Medical School. To stay out of debt, he had committed himself to serve in the Air Force Reserve. The Air Force would pay his medical school debt if he completed his residency, plus another year of service in a public health service hospital. Billy had recently started his residency program in a public health service hospital in San Francisco. He had been in the program for the past two weeks, working 100 hours per week. This was his first day off, and Patty and their boys were driving up from Tucson to join him. He had told her he would have a place for them to live, and he was hoping we could help them find that place quickly.

Billy seemed to be open, honest, and a wholehearted follower of Jesus. He was candid about his life and direct about his faith. I liked him right away. While Billy was still in my office, I went to the phone and called Cheryl Morrison. I knew she and her husband Sev were going on vacation with their children for a couple of weeks. I asked Cheryl if it would be possible for the Stocktons to use their home while they were gone. She and Sev were happy to open their home to a family in need.

My next call was to Jan Dow, a realtor in our church. I asked Jan if she could help the Stocktons find a house to rent in the next two weeks. When Patty and the boys arrived the next day, they went straight into the Morrisons' four-bedroom, ranch-style home.

Jan came over during the week, met Patty, and the ladies drove around town until they found a home to rent.

In the following months, Kristina and I became good friends with Billy and Patty. Matthew became friends with Peter and John Stockton. Philip and David Stockton were just learning to walk, but they eventually became friends as well. We had no idea how important these relationships would be to both families in the coming decades.

The Stocktons got as involved in the Novato church as they could, considering Billy was still working 80 to 100 hours a week in the residency program. Patty was an excellent Bible teacher. She started a women's Bible study that became popular with many young mothers. As our congregation got to know Billy, he had more people consulting with him after our services, than with our pastors. He was a gifted doctor, and he didn't mind giving free advice or treatment to our church members.

Billy loved to fish, just like Kristina and me. We took our families on fishing vacations together to Lake Tahoe and the Feather River.

On one fishing trip, Billy and I took his three boys and my two sons, along with a troubled teenager named Joey Lawrence. Joey had once been busted for setting our local junior high school on fire. I wasn't too keen on taking Joey, but Billy thought we could help him. He wanted to share Christ with Joey and expose him to fishing and camping. Billy was bigger than me, stronger than me, and impossible for me to reason with once he had his mind made up. Joey was coming on our fishing trip whether I liked it or not.

On the first day of the trip, we drove five hours north and west to Burney, California, one of the premier trout fishing areas in America. We stopped to camp along a beautiful stream. The boys jumped out of the van and started running around the camp as soon as we parked. As Billy and I were setting up our tent, I heard Joey ask, "Do you have any tape?"

I turned around. Joey had a big butcher knife in one hand and a long branch in his other hand.

"What do you think you're doing with that? Give me that knife right now!" I demanded as I pulled the knife from Joey's hands.

"I want to get a fish." he replied.

"These are native trout. They are hard to catch even when you have a fishing pole and know what you're doing. You can't get one of these trout with a knife on a stick!"

"But I want to try," Joey pleaded.

"Go ahead and let him try," Billy commanded me.

I couldn't believe Billy wasn't backing me up. "There is no way he can get a trout with that knife, and I don't want him hurting someone!" I replied, defending myself.

"Let him try. It won't hurt anything."

So, while we continued to set up camp, Joey went off to fish with his knife taped to a branch. He was back in camp a half hour later, carrying two big trout he had speared. Someone learned something about swallowing pride that day, and it wasn't Joey Lawrence.

Years later, I discovered that Joey had become my brother Barry's neighbor. I talked with Joey on the steps of his condo in Novato. He was married with four children and following the Lord with his wife. We recalled our camping trip and how he had speared the trout. Sadly, Joey died from a brain tumor when he was still in his thirties. His life was short but fruitful. Part of the credit goes to Billy Stockton, who loved Jesus enough to share his life with a troubled teenager.

Speaking Up for Biblical Principles

One day, a mother in our church called to tell me that the required reading book in her daughter's fourth grade public school class included a story with a prayer to the devil. The book had several other objectionable parts as well, but the prayer to the devil had pushed this mother over the edge. She had gone to the school and talked with the teacher about the book, but the teacher was adamant that she would continue to use it. She told me she was going to take the issue to the school board and asked if I would accompany her.

This issue was the focus of my first trip to the school board. I didn't want to be a stereotypical pastor ranting against a book with a minor transgression in it. I was aware that teachers hated censorship. However, if we couldn't reason with a teacher or the school board over an issue as flagrant as devil worship, what could we ever speak out against? We were not being the salt and light in our community Jesus told us to be if we were afraid to confront evil.

So, we went to the school board and politely tried to explain why a book like this was inappropriate for fourth graders. We were not well received. They sided with the teacher and didn't seem to appreciate our concerns at all. A few months later, another issue came to my attention. This time, the school board was considering a motion to allow girls who were twelve and older to be released from school to get an abortion without their parents' permission. This issue really upset me. Parents needed to give permission for their children to go on field trips anywhere outside of the school grounds, even to a local museum. Yet, this proposal declared their permission wasn't needed for their daughters to get an abortion. I thought this position was contrary to common sense and harmful to the children they were supposed to be educating.

Many concerned parents attended the school board meeting the night the abortion issue was to be discussed. The room was filled with tension. We sat patiently for an hour and a half while board members addressed other items on their agenda. They seemed to be hoping we would all go home before the abortion issue was presented. When the time came to address their abortion policy, several of us spoke out. My heart was beating rapidly when I began. I tried to speak slowly and without anger, using my prepared remarks:

> *How can the school board ignore the need for parental permission when a child is seeking an abortion? To have a child, put a child up for adoption, or have an abortion are some of the most serious decisions a young woman will ever make in her life. Twelve-year-old girls are not responsible enough to make decisions of this magnitude apart from their parents. I believe all babies growing in their mothers' wombs should be protected, not aborted. I realize that our laws give mothers freedom to abort their babies. However, the school has a*

responsibility to support the institution of the family, not circumvent it, regardless of whether some parents might react poorly to their daughter's pregnancy. It is most likely that a girl's parents will react in support of her, and that their support will be very helpful in the serious decision their daughter is going to make. Parents send their children to school and trust that they will remain in school all day unless they are notified differently. Anything to circumvent the trust that parents place in the school would be a violation of the parents' rights to guide their children.

I wanted the board to know this was a life-and-death decision, and they had the responsibility to help children connect with their parents, not hide the critical issues of their lives from them. However, the board did not seem to appreciate my comments or the comments several other concerned parents made that night. They voted to allow girls who were twelve and older to be released from school for abortions without their parents' knowledge or consent. They made us feel like we had no place in their decision-making process. From that night on, I realized we might have to start our own school to educate our children. The beginning of wisdom is the fear of the Lord. It didn't seem to me that the leaders of the Novato Unified School District had the beginning of wisdom.

A few weeks after my second encounter with the school board, I was standing on the sidelines at a Novato High School football game. As I watched the game, the superintendent of schools came over and stood beside me. He was a tall gentleman who looked down on me in more ways than one. He had not appreciated me going to the school board and making my concerns public. He told me he was a Presbyterian, and he had different views than I did. He asked me where I had gone to seminary. I told him I had not gone to seminary. His sneer made it clear that he didn't think I was qualified to be a pastor, let alone try to tell him how to run the school district.

My encounter with the superintendent helped clarify something in my heart. I had spent a lot of time meditating on the words of the Apostle Paul in 2 Corinthians 3:4–6:

> And such confidence we have through Christ toward God. Not that we are adequate in ourselves to consider anything as coming from ourselves, but our adequacy is from God, who also made us adequate as servants of a new covenant, not of the letter, but of the Spirit; for the letter kills, but the Spirit gives life.

I was qualified to preach and teach the Word of God not because I went to seminary; my adequacy came from God through Christ. The grace of Christ qualifies everyone who serves the Lord. Education can be very helpful, but confidence is essential. Confidence in God comes because Jesus makes us competent. I am also confident that standing up for the rights of parents and unborn children is pleasing to God.

One afternoon, Kent and Bob Hymers came by my house to talk. They wanted me to sign a document Kent had written pointing out errors in the teachings of Bob Mumford, Don Basham, Charles Simpson, and Ern Baxter. Those men, along with Derek Prince, were originally based in Fort Lauderdale.

After one of their friends had fallen into immorality, they had formed covenant relationships to help strengthen each other to resist the temptations and overcome the challenges of public ministry. They were the founders and teachers of *New Wine* magazine, which I subscribed to and read each month. I also had attended several of their public meetings and conferences over the years, which had been very inspiring. I considered them gifted Bible teachers. Even though I didn't agree with the way they applied the principles of submission and authority, I still respected them. Their teachings had helped me grow spiritually and given me understanding of God's kingdom. I wasn't about to sign my name to Kent's paper.

Kent and Bob grew angry when I told them I wasn't going to sign the paper. They tried to pressure me. They told me I was being rebellious. They told me I was naïve. They tried to convince me that the Fort Lauderdale men were intent on duping me into joining their movement. As the discussion heated up, I tried to reaffirm my loyalty to our Open Door churches, but I wouldn't sign their paper. Bob told Kent that he should remove me from leading the church in Novato. Bob didn't realize that the Novato Open Door was loyal to me. Kent couldn't fire me even if he wanted to. Nevertheless, it was very upsetting to hear Bob suggest it.

I loved Kent, although we had grown distant from each other the last few years. Something in him had changed. When I dropped by his house unannounced to pick up Kristina for a date in the early '70s, I would often hear him singing praise songs to the Lord. These days it was more common to overhear him upset with someone than singing praise songs.

By the time Kent and Bob left my house, I was really shaken. I wasn't about to renounce the Florida teachers who had helped me grow in the Lord, even if they had problems. Neither did I want to be at odds with Kent and Bob. Bob had been one of the founders of our church in San Rafael, and Kent had been the closest thing to a spiritual father I had in the early days of my walk with the Lord. I attended his Bible studies for two years. He prayed for me to be filled with the Holy Spirit and gave me good counsel, which helped me stay out of cults. He had provided a home for Kristina when her parents left the country when she was only seventeen. I loved him, but we were now in a battle that really disturbed me.

I decided to go on a two-week fast. I would often fast when I felt like I needed a spiritual breakthrough. I knew I needed one now. I was caught between two groups of warring believers who I loved. I worked with the Open Door pastors, but I gained a lot of help from the teachers who published *New Wine* magazine. I knew this was a pivotal time in my life and ministry. I needed the Lord to help me fight this battle in the Spirit.

The first week I ate no food and drank only water. After seven days, my friend Jerry Westfall came to visit from Mendocino. Jerry and I loved playing tennis, so we went out to play a couple of sets. Hoping to at least make it competitive, I drank some fruit juice before we began. It didn't help much since I was still too weak to play well. Jerry beat me soundly and later published his winning score in his newsletter. After he left, I resumed fasting for another week.

One night during the second week of my fast, I had a profound dream. A face like an angel of the Lord appeared in my dream. I stared at the face and heard these words: *"Spiritual authority is in Me."* When I awoke, I knew the Lord had spoken to me. I didn't need to join Bob Mumford and his leaders to have spiritual authority, nor did I need to obey Kent's command to renounce them in order to be right with God. Spiritual authority is found in Jesus Christ. If I abide in Him, I am secure. I need my life to be rooted and grounded in Christ. He will help me fight any battles I face, because Jesus is Lord of Lords and King of Kings.

Bob Hymers went back to Los Angeles. It would be several years before we reconciled. Kent never pressured me to sign his paper again. And nobody tried to remove me from the church. The storm passed, and the revelation remained. It was an important turning point for me as a pastor and a man of God. It also helped prepare me for the spiritual battles that broke out in the Open Door Commission a year later.

I've never considered myself a good counselor, because I'm usually too impatient to hold back what I'm thinking when people explain their problems to me. I *"do unto others as I would have them do unto me."* I like people to be direct and tell me what they really think and feel. I am very direct, especially when I'm counseling someone. One afternoon, I learned a good lesson about human nature from a young man who came to me for counseling.

As I was talking with this young man for the first time, I asked if there was anything he needed to confess to the Lord. He thought for a moment and then told me he did need to confess something. He explained he had once stolen hubcaps from a car. I nodded when he made the confession, and then asked if there was anything more. After a minute, he admitted he had taken the tires from the car as well. I paused again.

He then mentioned that he took the steering wheel too. When I didn't react with surprise, he finally admitted that the hubcaps, tires, and steering wheel were attached to the car. He had stolen the car and wanted to see how upset I would get before he told me the entire story. We prayed together, but this was the last time I saw him.

I don't have a lot of grace for counseling people, but God gave me grace to lead a wonderful church in Novato. Slowly but surely, we kept growing as the Lord added new believers to our congregation. I thought a growing congregation with new people committing their lives to Jesus every week was normal for a church. At the time, I thought the way our members loved one another and how they stayed faithful in their marriages was the way all Christians lived.

In the years to come, I would learn that our fellowship at the Open Door in Novato was blessed by God in a wonderful way. It's not that other churches never experienced the type of love and blessings we were experiencing, because many others do as well. It was more the special nature of God's kingdom, which was powerfully manifesting in our lives during that season.

We had lived through what church historians would later call The Jesus Movement. We had been in the midst of a revival, which we considered normal Christianity. Often, those who experience great blessings are tested by great trials. Many of the people and the pastors of our church, myself included, would experience great trials in the years to come. The trials would come, not because we didn't love the Lord or because we had made some mistake. We were young, inexperienced, and naïve, but we were on a journey toward heaven.

Our individual journeys would take each of us in directions we would not have imagined at the time. However, it brings me great joy to know that most of the people who were on that journey with us then are still following the Lord to this day.

In the summer of 1978, Bob Pangburn took Kristina and me to a museum in Utica, New York, where I was captivated by four paintings called "The Voyage of Life," by Thomas Cole. The first painting showed a young child resting in a gondola while an angel guided the gondola along a tranquil river through an Eden-like setting.

In the second painting, the boy had grown into a young man. He was now guiding the gondola along a wider river toward a bright heavenly kingdom in the far distance. The angel was standing on the bank of the river waving good-bye. He knew the young man was going to encounter great challenges as he pursued his destiny, but it was his time to guide the gondola.

In the third painting, the river had become a raging torrent. The angel was barely discernible in distant storm clouds in one upper corner of the painting. The devil was looming in the storm clouds in the other corner. A middle-aged man was praying as his gondola careened toward boulders. The heavenly kingdom was no longer visible. The outcome of the man's life was shrouded in danger and uncertainty.

In the fourth painting, the river had become quiet. A hovering angel was welcoming an old man as his gondola approached the heavenly kingdom.

I was like the young man in the second painting when I saw these pictures. I had vision, faith, and hope for the future. I thought I knew where I was going and what was ahead of me. I was about to meet challenges that would test me beyond what I had ever imagined. I'm ending this book at this point, which may seem abrupt. My next book will tell the stories of the unexpected trials and challenges I faced, which the third painting represents.

I'm honored you took the time to read about my life. I know you have your own stories. I hope my experiences will encourage you to share your stories as well. As you journey toward heaven, bring others with you. If you serve Jesus and obey His words, He will reveal Himself to you, and your reward will be great.

APPENDIX A
Chapters and Chapter Subheaders

ACKNOWLEDGMENTS

When I was a troubled teenager, my mother, Roberta Buckley, always kept her home open to me. Her faith and love helped rescue me from deep confusion and depression. I am also thankful for my dad, John Buckley, who encouraged me, even when his own soul was shrouded in pain.

This book has been edited with loving input from Debbie Becker, Linda Barkman, Carla Bruce, Maddie Middelstaedt, and Pauly Heller. Chris Schoenleb shaped my stories into a cohesive narrative. Margie Wilson edited all our work into a finished book.

I also want to thank my many friends in the Open Door Churches in California and at Living Streams in Phoenix who have prayed for me and blessed our family for years. I am sorry I wasn't able to tell your story in this book and give you personal credit for the love you have shown for the Lord.

For those friends who have urged me to write this book over the years, thank you. I needed to be told over and over that this was something the Lord wanted me to do. You were used to prod me into obedience, and I am grateful for your loving encouragement.

I am also grateful for my brothers and sisters: John Buckley, Barry Buckley, Robert Buckley, Kim Stafford, Susan Fisher, Katie Long, and Beth Buckley. I wish I had been a more loving big brother to you when we were growing up.

And, I am very proud of my children Phil Buckley, Kelly Buckley, and Kathryn Buckley. They have lived through a lot of pain in their lives and have emerged as adults who bless and encourage everyone who knows them.

Matthew Buckley is my greatest inspiration. He is present with Jesus and inspires my heart from heaven.